IT'S A COP'S LIFE

By George Vuilleumier

RoseDog Books

PITTSBURGH, PENNSYLVANIA 15222

ISBN # 0-8059-9937-X

Printed in the United States of America

First Printing

For information or to order additional books, please write:
RoseDog Books
701 Smithfield Street
Third Floor
Pittsburgh, Pennsylvania 15222
U.S.A.
1-800-834-1803

Or visit our website and online catalogue at www.rosedogbookstore.com

This book is dedicated to my wife of 52 years who was convinced this book would never be published and our loving daughter Cheryl, President of my fan club, a membership of one (Two including our family cat Omar).

<u>ONE</u>

I was freezing. I had on a heavy foul weather jacket, gloves and a watch cap pulled down over my ears. But at ten degrees below zero in the North Atlantic, my teeth were chattering. I was standing amid ship on the starboard side as the U. S. Coast Guard Cutter *Snohomish* fought her way in a white-capped sea toward her homeport of Rockland, Maine. She was making slow headway because of her burden a sinking fishing trawler tied to her starboard side (that's the right side for all you landlubbers) with three-inch hawsers. Although the crew of the trawler had been transferred to the safety of the *Snohomish's* mess deck to thaw out, their captain was still below deck trying desperately to save his boat. About an hour previously, our boatswain mate had stationed me to my post, handed me one of the ship's fire axes and said, "Kid, if this trawler starts to go down, yell to the captain down there to get the hell out and then chop us free or the damned trawler will take us down with her." I replied, "Gotcha Boats." I couldn't quite imagine that trawler dragging down our 110-foot cutter/ice breaker that resembled a tug-boat more than a sleek cutter, but I was a new kid on the block so to speak, and I didn't comment further. The *Snohomish*, which was affectionately referred to by her crew as "The Mighty S," had a top speed of only about 16 to 17 knots but ably had enough power to pull a freight train.

As I stood there clutching that fire axe and pondering about the overwhelming responsibility given to an 18-year-old just two weeks out of boot camp, I began to reflect on how I had arrived at this new station of my life. I concluded that it had been by my choice. Only two weeks previous, I had graduated from the Coast Guard's boot camp located at the mouth of the Delaware River in Cape May, New Jersey. In an exit interview, after look-ing through my file, noting that I had played trombone in my high school band and orchestra, had played in a local dance band called *The Music Makers,* and at one time even had my own combo, the instructor remarked that the Coast Guard was in the process of forming a new marching band and was also contemplating the formation of a dance band. He asked me if I would be interested in being permanently assigned to the Cape May Base and participating as a musician. Since I probably had read every sea story in my high school library and envisioned a seafaring experience only to be matched by a Hollywood movie, I probably stuck my chest out as I responded, "Sir. I joined this outfit to go to sea, not to play trombone." Boy! Did they ever oblige me. Now, standing on the deck of the *Snohomish,* freezing my you know what off, I thought of how I could have been sitting in a nice warm auditorium in New Jersey emptying the spit valve on my trombone.

As a young man coming from an average middle class family, who had never really been that far from home, boot camp on the Atlantic Ocean in the dead of winter had been an awakening if not shocking experience. I'd had my head scalped like you wouldn't believe, issued dungarees designed for WACS (female members of Coast Guard during World War II) and shoes that caused so many blisters I ended up wearing only galoshes through most of my boot camp training and after being issued two buckets in which to hand wash my clothes to be hung outside the barracks on strings tied in square knots if you will. I was not a happy seaman apprentice. To make matters worse, I could not adjust to institutional food. Although it was probably very nutritious, like many other kids coming from a middle class family, I had been spoiled rotten by my mother who like most people those days, had no conception of nutrition but to me was a good cook. Her philosophy was the more you ate, the healthier you were and I ended up with a weight problem which now boot camp was resolving for me. Growing up in the 1930s depression, my father found little work as a carpenter, often shoveling snow in the winter to survive and we were dirt poor. But my sister, six years my elder, and I didn't know it. We were never hungry and I always had a toy to play with. We had been blessed with a very loving mother and father and had enjoyed a happy childhood, spending all our summers in York Beach, Maine where my mother grew up and our grandmother still lived.

We even had a summer home in York Beach. At least it was a summer home to us anyway. Actually it was a two-story garage sided and roofed in corrugated steel. The second floor served as our living quarters, half of which held stored lumber from my grandfather's former business as a building contractor. The remaining area (we didn't have rooms) held three iron beds, a table and a kitchen without running water which had to be hauled from elsewhere. Kerosene lamps substituted for electricity but from the rickety porch we could actually see the ocean at Short Sands Beach. The lower half of the structure held more of my grandfather's stored lumber and for a bathroom, a "two holer" on a dirt floor. But to my sister and me, this was total bliss. Having arrived from our home in Newton, Massachusetts in a borrowed car (we had none in those days) I enjoyed every summer with mornings on the beach and afternoons building "stuff" with my grandfather's handy lumber. Somehow my dad was able to spend most weekends with us. And with his patience, I learned to swim shortly after I learned to walk. Even with water temperatures averaging 60 to 65 degrees. During the summers, my grandmother lived next door in what could only be described as another shack but with running water and electricity. Although she had four other grandchildren, my grandmother and I became very close over the years. In fact I spent every school vacation, hitchhiking to York Beach to spend time with her, including Thanksgiving as she lived alone. My grandfather who had been a very successful contractor in York during the 1920's building the movie theater, the bowling alley and many other prominent buildings which still stand today and was a deputy sheriff as well. But he had long since run off with a secret lover to Connecticut. When I was small I looked at him as my first hero and never tired of my grandmother's stories about him such as when he was a deputy sheriff and captured an escaped prisoner from the nearby Portsmouth Navy Yard, handcuffed him to my grandmother and proceeded off to capture a second escapee. She never showed her bitterness over his infidelity and never bad-mouthed him in front of her grandchildren.

When still assigned to the *Snohomish*, I managed to get back to my home in Newton about every other month and always stopped for a visit with my grandmother in York Beach, often at 2:00 AM or even 3:00 AM. I would knock on her unlocked door and yell up to her bedroom, "Grandma, its me—Jed," her private nickname for me. She would come down stairs and we would enjoy a cup of tea and one of her homemade blueberry muffins and then I would be on my way to Massachusetts.

<u>TWO</u>

A young man, I found, matures rather quickly in the military and the *Snohomish* advanced my maturity rather rapidly. In my two and a half years there I participated in 57 air sea rescue missions. Most involved fishing trawlers who chose to ride out one of the vicious storms in the North Atlantic and fill their holds with fish before heading back to their various ports thereby showing a profit rather than return with a loss for the owner of the vessel and its crew. I know of no heartier or tougher breed than Maine fishermen. Often exposed to severe weather and poor working conditions, one had to admire their tenacity and work ethic.

Coast Guardsmen always enjoyed a special bond with fishermen as they relied heavily on us for their safety and we could always depend on them for assistance if anyone had a problem ashore. I can recall on one occasion, the Snohomish tied up for the night in Southwest Harbor, Maine, another small coastal town consisting of a Congregational church, a gas station and maybe a convenience store in the town's center. Two of my shipmates and I, having been given liberty, decided to brave a snowstorm and venture up to the local movie theater. When the movie was over, we trudged back in the snow to the dock where the *Snohomish* had been moored but to our surprise, the ship was not there. She had been called out on yet another rescue mission. There was no available shelter there for us and we envisioned standing in that storm all night trying to keep from freezing. At an adjacent dock we saw a trawler tied up with her mast lit. A crew of six fishermen were on board and we spent the night drinking hot coffee and eating fried fish, totally enjoying their companionship until the *Snohomish* returned to pick us up at daylight the next morning.

Normally, when we received a call from a trawler, always in a rough sea and often at night, our procedure was to have the Rockland fire horn

4

sound to alert those on liberty. They had 30 minutes to get back on board and off we went to the rescue mission. Some missions took us as far north as Halifax, Nova Scotia, on the Canadian border. Many years later, the Coast Guard used larger vessels, limiting the *Snohomish* to Maine waters. Just as well I think as I have seen 30-degree rolls and it's only 45 degrees to the level of the sea's surface. I have seen waves covering the ship's bridge.

During a hurricane in 1949, we were dispatched to retrieve an unoccupied yacht which had slipped its mooring in Booth Bay Harbor and was considered a navigational hazard. As we proceeded out to sea with only half the crew aboard, I was at the helm and the weather became so violent, I heard our Captain radio Coast Guard Headquarters in Boston advising that the hurricane was endangering the ship and the lives of its crew. He requested that we be allowed to turn back to our base in Rockland and it was granted. I thought to myself, "Oh shit!" At the time, the Captain and I were the only members of the crew who were not violently seasick. When I was finally relieved from the helm I made my way to my bunk below and suddenly became very ill myself. As it worked out, there is a sea wall that extends out over a mile protecting the entrance to Rockland Harbor and the ocean was still very choppy. Our captain feared with a 100 mile per hour wind blowing, we would end up on the rocks, so we ended up riding out the hurricane at sea. When we finally tied up at our base, I swore to myself that I would never go to sea again and may never even drink water again either. ..

Of the 57 air sea rescues I participated in while assigned to "The Mighty S," there was no loss of life involved except the rescue we never got to. It still haunts me even today. We were in port and I had the midnight to four AM watch on the bridge. The weather was really nasty. About 2:00 AM, I heard over the ship's radio a frantic voice call "Mayday, Mayday, Mayday. This is the trawler *Gudium* and we are sinking." The caller then gave the vessel's latitude and longitude. I frantically jotted it down and tried to call the *Gudium* but could get no answer. Although Coast Guard Headquarters in Boston had a much more powerful transmitter, they were not picking up the *Gudium's* desperate call. Both our Captain and his Exec were home ashore at our base in Rockland. I felt I had to do something. The only telephone available was on shore at our base. I hustled up the gangplank to the office which of course was closed and all locked up. Fearing disciplinary action would probably result, I still broke the office door window gaining entrance to the office and telephoned Coast Guard Boston, giving them the *Gudium's* position. They immediately dispatched help from the nearest cutter but when the Coast Guard arrived, all they found was some debris. The trawler's crew had gone to a watery grave. Incidentally, I was verbally commended for my quick action and promised some kind of recognition but Coast Guard being Coast Guard, it never came and I doubt it was ever recorded in my file.

Another rescue ended up on a much more positive note. There was and still is a lighthouse located about 30 miles out to sea from Rockland, Maine named Matinicus Rock and it is exactly that. In fact it was then manned by Coast Guardsmen who ordered their supplies from the Coast Guard base in Rockland every month. The head lighthouse keeper routinely ordered a lawn mower even though Matinicus Rock does not have a blade of grass. It was just his way of coping with boredom, adding a little humor to his life. Matinicus Rock is probably the most isolated lighthouse on the coast of Maine and now, like all other lighthouses, it is automated.

One morning we were notified by Coast Guardsmen on Matinicus Rock, that they were observing through binoculars, a dory containing six men about two or three miles north of the lighthouse. This was immediately after another North Atlantic storm had passed and the ocean was still very choppy. We immediately proceeded to the location of the small boat, finding six fishermen whose trawler had sunk during the night and for some reason were unable to call for help. I will never forget the faces of those six men when we pulled along side to scoop them up. They were convinced that they would have never survived in that small boat for any given period of time. As any seaman or boat enthusiast will tell you, that black and white Coast Guard vessel with the orange stripe on the side of its hull is always a welcome sight to all except of course the drug dealers and smugglers.

Along with our air sea rescue responsibilities, the *Snohomish* was equipped as an icebreaker. So during the winter, oil tankers traveled up the Penobscot River towards Bangor or the Kennebec River towards Augusta, Maine's capital and a winter freeze would suddenly hit. As everyone knows, when water freezes and turns to ice, it expands and the outer skins of oil tankers are very thin, causing ice to crush against them with a potential for an oil spill. So tankers were really relieved to see "The Mighty S" chugging toward them so that they could again negotiate the river without fear of damaging their ship.

THREE

As previously mentioned, all lighthouses are now automated, but in those days they were operated by Coast Guardsmen and lighthouse keepers. Many lighthouses in Maine have no direct access to the mainland and all the fuel and other provisions had to be delivered by boat. So periodically provisions would be requested from the Rockland Coast Guard Base and delivered by the *Snohomish*, often in rough weather. All lighthouses were and still are surrounded by rocks and have maybe a small slip for access. When the *Snohomish* arrived at a particular lighthouse, she would drop anchor maybe a half mile away and provisions would be rowed in by our Monamoy lifeboat. (No rafts with outboard motors in those days, folks.) The sea was often choppy and presented quite a challenge. Fuel was carried in 50-gallon drums and delivered by hauling barrels from the *Snohomish's* deck, rigged by ropes to the lighthouse, pulling them across the water by hand. Again, no winches or hoists.

One day, two high ranking officers from Coast Guard Headquarters in Boston, dawned our decks, saying they had a need to inspect Matinicus Rock. Although it was springtime with plenty of sunshine, there was still a heavy sea running. When we arrived at Matinicus Rock, they were told they would be transported to the lighthouse by way of the ship's hand rowed lifeboat. They took one look, declined the offer and returned to the safety of their desks in Boston.

The *Snohomish's* captain and I were not the best of friends. Although a very qualified seaman and an accomplished navigator, I found his personality often difficult to fathom. To digress, one bright sunny morning, we headed out to sea and he was sharply dressed in his freshly starched tan uniform with a clean cover on his uniform hat. As he stepped out onto the wing of the bridge, a sea gull flew over and let go, depositing white material directly on the skipper's hat. Perfect aim in my view. He calmly looked up at the sea gull and remarked to no one in particular, "A lot of people around here would like to do that." I muttered to myself, "You got that right, Skipper."

May I point out at this point in my saga, that although the North Atlantic Ocean can be brutal weather-wise, especially during the winter months, biased as I probably may be, I think the Maine coastline is second to none in the world in beauty or scenery. Its shores are rocky with a few beautiful beaches suited for swimming. It is dotted with numerous islands and inlets, all with tall Maine spruce and pine trees and plenty of wildlife including a heavy population of moose. One cannot adequately describe its beauty, particularly during the autumn season when its forests glow with color.

But winter in the North Atlantic can be brutal working rescue missions, pulling frozen hawsers across the deck at all hours of the night, little sleep and too much partying on shore liberty. It finally caught up with me. In those days the medical care for those aboard was limited to a bottle of aspirin in the captain's medicine cabinet. The only available aid was a civilian contract doctor in Camden, about eight miles from Rockland. Realizing I was one sick sailor, I reported to the doctor for any possible assistance I could get. He took my temperature which was 104 degrees and wrote our captain a notice that I was to be admitted to the Portland Marine Hospital for treatment, immediately if not sooner .. When I returned to the *Snohomish* and gave our captain the doctor's notice, his only remark was, "I'm short handed enough now. I'll take care of you whenever you get back." I interpreted this as a veiled threat of retribution which did not help my condition any. How I ever made it, driving 80 miles to the Portland Marine Hospital, I'll never know. They say that the Good Lord watches over cops and drunks but I am convinced he watches over sailors too, at least Coast Guardsmen. At any rate, I was diagnosed as having an ulcerated throat condition, my tonsils showing actual holes in them. I spent the next 30 days in the Portland Marine Hospital with penicillin being pumped into me until I became immune to it. I must point out that our captain did pay me a visit and talked to the physicians but I often wondered if he was just making sure I was where I was supposed to be. Upon my release, I returned to the *Snohomish* with some apprehension but no retaliation was ever shown and life aboard the *Snohomish* continued as before.

After two and a half years on the *Snohomish*, for some reason not known to me, I had not been promoted to Seaman 1st, E-3 and had decided to request a transfer. Upon receiving my request, our captain called me into the chartroom and said he would either approve my transfer or promote me to Seaman 1st, E-3. My choice. Thinking I would in all probability be promoted wherever I was transferred to, I chose to opt for the transfer. The result? I was promoted with no transfer approved.

Subsequently, our captain was reassigned and our new skipper arrived. He was a good officer and became very well liked. At that time, and I understand is still the case, the Coast Guard had a policy in effect called "mutual-transfers" wherein if two Coast Guardsmen of the same rank wished to switch posts of duty at their own expense, with the approval of their respective commanding officers, it would be allowed. As luck would have it, in their magazine published periodically entitled *Coast Guard* (very original, don't you think?), I read where a Seaman 1st Class E-3 assigned to the Coast Guard Base in Key West, Florida was looking for a mutual transfer near his home in Rockland, Maine where the *Snohomish* was stationed.

I couldn't believe my good fortune. I approached our new skipper and both he and the commanding officer in Key West approved the transfer. So in May of 1951, my time in the North Atlantic having been served, I packed my sea bag with all my worldly possessions and headed for Key West.

FOUR

Welcome to South Florida, George. Having never personally seen a palm tree and with all that glorious sunshine around, I was indeed impressed. So impressed, I decided to take a little time off when I went through Miami Beach and soak up some Florida sun for a couple of days. That was a mistake. After spending just one morning laying in that Florida sun with my snow white skin, especially with the ultraviolet rays being so strong in May, I ended up with such a severe sunburn I couldn't even get my starched white uniform on. It was so painful I sought medical attention at the Coast Guard Headquarters for their 7th District, located in Coral Gables nearby. But I was refused any medical help based on their rationale that my sunburn was due to my own carelessness and any treatment would result in my enlistment being extended. So I painfully continued on my 168-mile journey to Key West, which under normal circumstances is an absolutely beautiful ride. One passes over several smaller keys and at one point a bridge seven miles long that separates the Atlantic Ocean from the Gulf of Mexico on the right. Did you know that Key West is closer to Havana, Cuba than it is to Miami and the U.S. mainland?

My assignment to Key West was a whole new world to me. At that time the civilian population consisted mostly of people of Cuban extraction. Key West boasted 3,000 sailors including a major submarine base, a Naval Air Station and 72 bars including the famous "Sloppy Joes." Our small Coast Guard station was located at the end of the submarine base adjacent to a marine aquarium complete with alligators. There were about a dozen Coast Guardsmen assigned, equipped with a 36 foot crash boat and a 50 foot utility boat that had three bunks for sleeping when at sea in the gulf. We had no facility for meals and were given extra per diem money for eating at the nearby Navy PX or a civilian restaurant. I was assigned to maintain the 38-foot crash boat and I was one happy sailor. Here I was, not 21 years of age and I had my own yacht. The crash boat was used mainly to retrieve Merchant Marine sailors passing by Key West on freighters and tankers who needed emergency medical attention. Occasionally we would be asked by the Navy to help search for fighter pilots when their Grummand Hellcats left over from World War II and probably obsolete by now, crashed in the Gulf of Mexico. We seldom found any pilots, only the plane on the ocean floor with the cockpit open indicating the pilot had been swept out to sea in the swift current of the Gulf of Mexico or the Atlantic Ocean.

I vividly remember one particular rescue mission involving a Navy eight passenger aircraft that when approaching its assigned airfield, developed engine problems, stalled and crashed into the Gulf with three Naval officers on board. When our crash boat arrived at the scene, we could see the airplane submerged in about 20 feet of water. One of the officers was floating upright, his clothing apparently snagged on a piece of wreckage below. He didn't appear to be conscious. Somehow we freed him from the wreckage and placed him on the deck of our craft. He was bleeding profusely with blood running down our gunnels. The impact had been so great, the seams in his boots actually exploded. It didn't look good.

As I was taking a break, leaning against the cabin, I noticed out of my peripheral vision his body slightly move. I attributed this to a nerve movement shortly after death. But as I looked, the man actually moved slightly. I yelled to a nearby Navy corpsman, "Hey! I think this one's still alive." He ran over and looked. He replied, "You're right." Immediate arrangements were made to transport the officer to a nearby Navy hospital and he survived. In fact, he may be still walking around today. I often wondered if he would ever want to fly again. The other two officers on board didn't make it.

While I was stationed in Key West, Harry Truman was president and maintained a getaway home on the Naval base. Quite often, I went to church on the base and would sit only six rows behind President Truman, his daughter Margaret and several Secret Service Agents assigned to his protection detail. It was Truman's habit when he came to town, to take early morning walks down Duval Street or one of the other streets nearby, accompanied by only a single Secret Service Agent. Of course he was well known to the local civilians and cheerfully waved at them. At the time, in addition to Coast Guardsmen, our station employed two or three civilian employees. One of them was a fellow nicknamed "Hap" for the happy person he always seemed to be. Hap, a native of Cuba, was the blackest man I have ever seen with the brightest blue eyes and he was a delight to be around. He was employed as a maintenance man and worked from 7:00 AM to 3:00 PM on our base. It seemed that every morning Hap would appear one hour early and fish off our dock for his evening dinner, thereby supplementing his meager civilian wages. One morning about 6:30 AM, Hap was sitting on the dock with his fishing pole and his peripheral vision noticed that a pair of white shoes had suddenly appeared along side him. Hap looked up and who was standing there but President Truman. Truman said, "You're not supposed to be working, are you?" and Hap replied, "No Sir. I don't start work until seven." The President smiled, patted Hap on the shoulder and continued on his way.

If you ever get a chance to visit Key West and the Florida Keys, I suggest you try to avoid doing so in July or August. Key West can be brutally hot. When I was there, it was before air conditioning was common and many a morning I would wake up in my bunk which only had a mattress cover, clad only in my shorts to find my mattress cover soaking with perspiration. I can recall standing once in the middle of Route U.S. 1, which I previously mentioned separates the Atlantic Ocean from the Gulf of Mexico, lighting a match and it didn't even flicker. There is often no breeze whatsoever in July or August as the trade winds are not stirring at that time of the year. But I was a happy sailor, enjoying six out of seven nights liberty. When I could afford the gas, I would spend the weekend in Miami with days on the beach, evenings at a local USO club or maybe nursing a couple of beers at a cocktail lounge. At night, I would park my convertible on Bicayne Boulevard and set my alarm clock on the dashboard to awaken me in time to feed the parking meter. (A practice I strongly recommend against these days.) Occasionally I would grab a spare bunk at Coast Guard Headquarters in Coral Gables and maybe if the opportunity arose, even grab a free meal there. Neither, of course, was authorized and somehow I still managed to end my Coast Guard career with the Good Conduct Medal. Looking back, I am now convinced this medal is not awarded for good conduct but for not getting caught.

However, while assigned to the Coast Guard station at Key West, I almost didn't make completing my enlistment. One day a Boatswain's Mate and I were assigned to head out in our 50-foot utility boat to the island of Dry Tortugus, located some distance out in the Gulf of Mexico. As any history buff might recall, Dry Tortugus Island adjacent to Fort Jefferson, is the largest brick fort in the United States, with walls eight feet thick and 50 feet high, where from 1865 to 1869 Dr, Samuel Mudd, who aided John Wilkes Booth after Booth assassinated President Abraham Lincoln, was incarcerated. Fort Jefferson also housed 2,000 Yankee prisoners during the Civil War. Fort Jefferson is now a national monument and Dry Tortugus Island is now a national park.

The reason "Boats" and I were sent to Dry Tortugas was to retrieve a buoy which had sunk in 30 feet of water, a mile or so off the island. Since I was considered a fairly accomplished swimmer and at one time even considered a career as a professional diver, our plan was to place our boat over the sunken buoy which was visible from the surface and I would swim down 30 feet, place the boat's winch hook around the buoy and haul it up into our boat. But when I reached the submerged buoy and wrapped the winch's hook around it, for some reason the winch slipped, catching my arm under the buoy, I knew I would be pinned under that buoy if I didn't get my arm free and I almost didn't. But the Good Lord didn't want me up there just yet and I finally freed my arm, bursting to the surface with my lungs screaming for air. I had no breathing device as the Coast Guard couldn't afford one. The Boatswain Mate's face was pure white. He could see what was going on with me and the buoy on the bottom of the Gulf and could do nothing about it. That wasn't my last diving experience but it sure was the scariest.

Life continued on in Key West and chuckling to myself, I thought that if I should ever personally meet President Truman around the neighborhood, so to speak, I would tell him what I thought about his extending my enlistment because of the Korean War. But it never happened. I didn't meet him and if I had I would probably limit our conversation to a "Good morning Mr. President." But now the Korean War was winding down and Truman had dropped the enlistment extension to six months, providing the individual enlisted in the Inactive Reserves for three years. Realizing that this country would have to be pretty desperate to reactivate a Seaman 1st Class E-3, I elected to be discharged. So in May of 1952, I reported for discharge at Coral Gables In an exit interview with a Chief Petty Officer, I was promised a promotion to 3rd Class Petty Officer if I reenlisted. I reminded the Chief that when I graduated from boot camp I was told that I qualified for almost every school the Coast Guard offered and it should be in my file. I said that although I had made numerous requests to attend one of their schools, my requests had gone unheeded. Thanks but no thanks. They had their chance. I suspect that I was even gloating at the time. So clutching my Honorable Discharge I walked out of the door as a civilian. Before I left Key West, two career Coast Guardsmen had cautioned me that I would never make it on the outside, that I would be back within a year. "Well," I thought, "we'll see."

FIVE

After buying my first new suit, I leisurely made my way back home to Newton, Massachusetts. At twenty-one, I felt I had the world by the tail .1 planned to take advantage of the Korean G.I. Bill and further my education. But realizing that scholastically, I had never been all that great as a student in high school (a better choice of words might be "lousy") I knew I'd need a year of prep school. I had already made arrangements to enroll at Chauncy Hall, a prep school for MIT (Massachusetts Institute of Technology). I had no interest in MIT and was leaning toward Boston University with a goal of becoming a disc jockey, no less. Having had at least some exposure to the music world, I had earlier considered attending the New England Conservatory of Music and a subsequent career with one of the big dance bands so popular in that era. But I concluded that being almost constantly on the road with one of the big bands, might not be too attractive after a few years, and I would end up a middle-aged man working in a music store somewhere. I guess my decision was a wise one as the big band era simply became too expensive and gradually disappeared, followed by rock music which I could never fathom. So I after one year of prep school Iopted for Boston University .t this point, I have not yet mentioned my interest in the opposite sex and lest some question of my manhood comes into anyone's mind, let me assure you I had a very healthy interest. Right after high school, a girl from York Beach, Maine and I had a very steady relationship. However, after completing boot camp I was reluctant to make a permanent commitment and we eventually parted company. Then there was a young lady in Rockland, Maine where the Snohomish was based. We had a very close relationship too but for some reason, I was uncomfortable. I felt there would always be a problem with fidelity which

14

was and still is very important to me. With my departure to Key West, we eventually went our separate ways.

There was also telephone operator from Waltham, Massachusetts, adjacent to my home in Newton, who was raised as an orphan and who constantly talked of having five or six kids. That scared the hell out of me. But having no consideration for my wallet, she insisted on dates that I could ill afford on a seaman's pay and although she actually visited me in Key West, I had come to classify her as someone who would never be financially responsible and would always remain a "gold digger." We also parted company.

And then there was Audrey! Over the years I had continued to correspond with my high school steady. Neither of us ever considered our relationship to be serious, mostly due to our difference in religion which we knew neither set of parents would ever accept. Anyway, she invited me to join our "old gang" at a New Years Eve party in 1949. I was on leave from the Snohomish at the time and was delighted.

When I knocked on the door, my old steady opened it and there was another girl standing there with her. Now I can't readily say I believe in love at first sight, but there stood the prettiest bit of feminine pulchritude I had ever seen. She had a gorgeous smile. Her name was Audrey and after graduation from Boston University, she worked with my old steady. Although my old steady was my date for that particular evening, I began to correspond with Audrey. When I was home on a weekend pass from the Snohomish, we often had simple dates like a movie or going dancing. She lived in Holbrook, some 23 miles from my home in Newton and her parents were good solid people, similar to mine. We continued to correspond while I was stationed in Key West and now that I was home again and had not seen Audrey for a year, we began to date again. We spent many a Sunday lying on the beach at Green Harbor on the south shore, enjoying each other's company.

SIX

Realizing I would be attending prep school in about four months and knowing that the Korean G.I. Bill only covered tuition and I would need at least some money, I went to work for Tulsa Williams building a natural gas line between Texas and Massachusetts. They paid top wages with plenty of overtime. Although I was making good money, I was working a 12 hour workday, six days a week and I was simply too tired at the end of the day to travel the 23 miles to Holbrook and Audrey. Gradually we stopped seeing each other. I completed prep school and entered Boston University the following fall.

I can only say I wasn't exactly thrilled with campus life. Having matured rather rapidly in the military, I did not feel very compatible with most students and to be honest, I missed Audrey. But without much enthusiasm, I continued on at Boston University, working part time as a cab driver on weekends to financially survive.

On Christmas Eve of 1952, I was still driving a cab but I had again called Audrey for a date, the following evening, December 26th. Audrey and I continued to see each other steadily and one year from December 26, 1952, we were married in the little Methodist church in Holbrook. A honeymoon followed in South Florida and I was even able to show off my new bride to my friends in Key West. We took up residence in a 27-foot mobile home that we had fornanced through Audrey's dad and he graciously allowed us to park it in their generous back yard. We then settled down to a married life.

Now I cannot say "and they lived happily ever after" as I am convinced that two people cannot suddenly live together in total bliss. Two separate personalities must learn to live together harmoniously and if both give

150%, it will work, and it did. I had decided that campus life wasn't for me and I needed a job but that wasn't easy. Audrey had a good job as a Service Representative with the telephone company and was making decent money even though she hated the work. I was unemployed for the first two months of our marriage and my macho ego had been bent out of shape. She was working and I was not. It bothered me and it showed. But eventually I found a job driving a lumber truck and although the pay wasn't very good and there was no overtime, my outlook did improve and so did our relationship.

After driving a lumber truck for a couple of months, one day someone from the Teamsters Union, unaware that I had found a job, notified me that Boston Sand and Gravel Company was looking for a cement mixer driver. I knew they were paying top money with plenty of overtime and I decided to apply. As I walked into the plant's office, I noticed one of their cement mixers parked outside. It looked like a monster to me. I had never even sat in a rig that big, let alone drive one. Luckily I happened to notice that the barrel on the rig was labeled "Jaguar" which meant nothing to me at the moment. When interviewed by the plant manager, he asked me if I had ever driven a mixer before. With all the confidence I could muster I said, "Oh Yeah." He said, "Where?" and I replied, "In the Army." Of course I had never in my life been in the Army let alone drive a cement mixer there but I knew that my reply could not immediately be traced. The manager's next question was "What kind of barrels did they have?" and I replied "Jaguars." He smiled and said, "Oh. We use Jaguars on our trucks too." I gave it my best "Oh, really?" The manager then summoned the driver of the mixer parked outside and pointing to me he said, "See what he can do, will you?" I hopped up into the passenger side of the rig and we were off with a load of cement to a construction sight in East Boston.

After unloading our cement in East Boston, we found a place to rinse out the barrel as not to do so would allow the cement residue remaining in the barrel to harden, making life for the driver miserable The driver then looked at me and said, "Okay kid, take us back to our plant in Cambridge." My stomach was flipping. As I climbed into the driver's seat, I looked at the ten speed transmission I was about to tackle, said a small prayer to myself and we were off in heavy traffic across the Mystic River bridge to the plant in Cambridge. I parked the rig near the office and followed the driver inside where I heard him tell the manager "He's okay." I had a job driving a cement mixer. Thank you Lord (I think).

I was now driving a cement mixer, learning the trade and making good money at it. One morning I was loading the barrel of my rig with cement. As I stood on the truck's platform, I noticed a scruffy looking old man watching me. He was wearing old baggy trousers and had a shirt on I

17

wouldn't wear washing our car. He was pointing to a valve on the mixer and shouting something to me but I couldn't hear him because of the cement pouring. I must have given him a rather annoyed look, waving him away. Why wasn't this old geezer sitting in a park somewhere playing chess? Later, I found out that scruffy old geezer was none other than the sole owner of Boston Sand and Gravel Company which included two cement plants, one in Cambridge and the other in Braintree and a fleet of about 50 cement trucks. I reflected that the next time I saw a scruffy old geezer I might show a little more diplomacy if not respect.

SEVEN

Even though I knew in my own mind that I really wouldn't be spending all my life driving a cement mixer, the money was great and I knew we could eventually save up enough money to accomplish our dream, a deposit on our first house.

Now I have always been fortunate in having my own clipping service. Her name is Audrey and while I will only scan a newspaper headlines and rely mostly on the morning or evening television news, even today Audrey reads the entire daily newspaper. So one evening early in the spring of 1954, I was probably watching some boring television show and as always, Audrey was sitting next to me reading the paper. Her remark to me was the same as it is now. "Did you see this?" She showed me a small one paragraph article entitled "Jobs in state police waiting." The article went on to say applications for enlistment in the Massachusetts State Police would be accepted until June 19th with a written examination scheduled for June 26th.

Now I must point out here that the Massachusetts State Police was, and still is, the most prestigious law enforcement agency in the Commonwealth. State Troopers were held in high esteem by the public. They were considered well disciplined, tough and nobody to mess with. With my Coast Guard background, I had at least in the back of my mind, given some thought about being in law enforcement but I knew it had to be as a state trooper. From what I had heard, getting through their academy was no easy task. We talked it over and I decided to try for one of the 50 positions open and I filed an application. The application was acknowledged and I was to report to the Charlestown Armory for an examination on June 26, 1954.

When I got to the armory there was a sea of other hopeful applicants. The exam took all morning long and was as tough as my college entrance examination, but longer. Inhibited by two tough looking state police sergeants walking steadily up and down the -aisles, I waded through the exam but ran out of time, leaving five or six questions unanswered. Like many examinations, I couldn't tell how I did but felt maybe not so hot.

Afterward, I walked in the door of our mobile home and said to Audrey, "I think I just wasted a perfectly good Saturday morning."

But thank heavens, I was wrong. I had passed the examination and was told to report for a physical exam and an oral board interview. I wasn't worried about the physical because I was in fairly good shape, but the oral board was something else. Surrounded by top-level state police brass, I again felt a little inhibited to say the least and the questions seemed to have gone on forever. As they say "The best speech you make is the one on the way home" and that's how I felt. According to the newspaper there had been 1,001 applications received for 50 trooper positions and by this time, I had put it all out my mind and was resigned to driving my cement mixer.

At about mid-morning on Thursday, July 29th, I was up on my rig's rear platform, busy pouring cement at the site of a new YMCA building being built in Quincy. As with most construction sites, the noise was deafening. Suddenly I felt a tug on the right leg of my jeans, I turned around to find Audrey with a big grin on her face, waiving a piece of paper at me. I had to read it three times before the contents sunk in on me. The first paragraph read, "This is to notify you that you have been selected to attend the Massachusetts State Police Academy as a Trainee." I was to report to the academy in Framingham on August 9th. Needless to say after that, I performed my duties as a cement mixer driver by rote as my mind was busy contemplating my new chosen career, or at least I hoped so.

At 10:00 AM on August 9th, I reported to the academy which at the time consisted of a bunch of Quonset huts located behind Troop A Headquarters on Route 9 in Framingham, Route 9 being the major artery between Boston, Hartford, Connecticut and New York City.

At our orientation I learned pretty much what I suspected. This was not going to be a piece of cake by any means. We were issued tan trainee uniforms and each of us assigned a bunk and a locker, all in one big Quonset hut room. The hours were from 5:30 AM until lights out at 10:00 PM, five and a half days a week. Saturday at noon, we would be allowed to "visit" our homes until 3:00 PM the next day, Sunday, but with a requirement that each week we would get a haircut. As one instructor put it, "I don't want to see any lice ladders."

The rest of that first day was to assure academy instructors that we were capable of doing what we certified on our original applications, that we could swim 500 yards. So off we went on a bus to a local college's swimming pool. We had our swimsuits with us per previous instructions so that was not a problem but the swimming was for some us. One by one, each of us entered the pool and swam the required 500 yards. All except three trainees who couldn't make it. In fact one went directly to the bottom of the pool. One trainee was the son of a police chief in a major city which must have been rather embarrassing for his father. At any rate, all three were immediately dismissed from the academy that evening. We all very quickly learned that these people at the academy were to be taken seriously. Apparently a year or so ago, a small child had been in trouble at a pond somewhere in Massachusetts and a state trooper attempting to rescue him had drowned in the process. The Commissioner of Public Safety, who has the ultimate responsibility for state police, did not want this type of incident to happen again and added the 500-yard swim requirement to the other qualifications.

Thus we spent the rest of our first week and part of the next, swimming, at a nearby pond, and I mean swimming. "Dutch" Holland was a civilian employed by the Red Cross. He was a certified Water Safety Instructor and in my mind, masochistic as well. Every morning we would spend 20 minutes swimming nonstop followed by a ten minute break while Dutch demonstrated strangle holds and other dangerous moves a drowning person might use. This was all very informative but guess who Dutch used as his subject? You guessed it. Somehow Dutch realized that I was an adequate swimmer and while everyone else was taking a break on the lawn. Dutch would yell out, "Vuilleumier! In the water!" He'd then use me as his victim. Everyone would get a break but me and even my classmates were expressing their sympathies when Dutch was not around. I would deliberately skip breakfast for fear of getting a gas cramp while Dutch, I was convinced, tried to drown me. But I found that when he put a strangle hold on me under the water, if I did not panic and kept my cool, I could break Dutch's stranglehold and surface with my "drowning person."

But in the end, we had the last laugh as Dutch mistakenly chose a 225 pound trainee who grew up on a pig farm in Leominster, to practice on. As Dutch dragged him to the bottom of the pond to further demonstrate how to get out of a drowning victim's stranglehold, the trainee panicked and scratched the living hell out of Dutch. The instructor took it as a personal assault and bitterly complained to our Commandant, but his complaint fell on deaf ears. It seemed our class had a new hero amongst us. I ended up with a Water Safety Instructor's Certificate. Big deal.

Then there was firearms training. We were issued Smith & Wesson six-inch revolvers, carried by all troopers at that time. The only experience I'd had with firearms was a 45 caliber semi-automatic during my Coast

Guard years and I couldn't hit a barn door with the dammed thing. In my first attempt at target shooting at the academy, I scored 17 out of 100, a pretty miserable effort I might add. The drill instructor, Bill "Gunny" Owen, a highly decorated U.S. Marine and a former drill instructor with the Marines, shook his head in disgust. But by the time I left the academy I had achieved Marksman status. "Gunny" and I are still good friends.

Other subjects included Massachusetts Criminal Law, Motor Vehicle Law, First Aid (always a bore to me), Officer Safety, and other subjects pertinent to our profession. We were only given one hour an evening to study for our tests that were given every Friday. If you failed to pass three tests, you were released from the academy. No one flunked.

The Massachusetts State Police Academy was designed, and I'm sure still is, as a combination Officers Candidate School such as the military has and a Marine Boot Camp. After the first few weeks, I started to feel the pressure and it showed. I missed my life with Audrey and began losing weight. I was having second thoughts about my new career and every Saturday noon when we started our brief time off, I was ready to quit. But when I did get back home, I found both my dad and Audrey's dad bragging all over town that their kid or son-in-law is in the State Police Academy and he's going to be a state trooper. I would never disappoint either of them and this caused me to reverse my attitude. I then swore to myself that the only way they would take me out of that academy would be in a box. I would make it if it killed me. And this got me through.

Unfortunately, our class had another setback. Somehow one of our trainees was stricken with polio. No vaccine had been developed at that time. Although he survived with no aftereffects, he was let go and was admitted to the next academy and subsequently enjoyed a long career as a trooper. Meanwhile, the rest of us were quarantined to the academy for the next weekend, thereby missing our 36 hours of time off. But as they say "misery loves company" and pulling together, we somehow got through that particular disappointment.

Our firearms training continued. At that time our Commissioner of Public Safety was Otis M. Whitney who also held the rank of Brigadier General in the National Guard. He thought it wise for us to spend a day at the U.S. Army's nearby Fort Devins for some training. We spent the morning receiving instruction in the use of both Rising and Thompson submachine guns, which were part of state police's arsenal and in fact we practiced with them both at the Army's firing range. In the afternoon, we were exposed to tear gas grenade training by a retired Army Lieutenant Colonel Johnson whom we immediately dubbed "Gashouse Johnson." Johnson was convinced that no one could be trained in the use of tear gas without personally being exposed to the stuff. So utilizing one of the Army's shacks on the range, in groups of six or seven, we were ordered into the shack and a gas grenade was lobbed in. Swell! Anyone who has ever been exposed to tear gas is aware of how debilitating it can be and we all received a heavy dose. Afterward, "Gashouse Johnson" seemed to feel that we were missing a trainee and inquired if we were all present. Someone yelled "There could be someone left in the shack," so Thompson investigated. Immediately some other wise guy lobbed in a grenade. Johnson came staggering out disoriented and furious. We all just smiled. Somehow, that made our day. We never saw "Gashouse Johnson" again but the fumes from that tear gas lingered in our clothing for a long time.

Our training also included the proper use and riding of motorcycles. I had never been on one before. Here we suffered a casualty. One of our classmates, negotiating a curve at the academy track, came around a corner facing a closed barn door. He froze at his controls and his motorcycle, at a reasonably high speed, crashed into the barn sending him up over the handlebars of his motorcycle severely damaging his lower extremities. Ouch! Huh? Unfortunately, he had to drop out. The rest of us managed to survive but in the years ahead, I did have a couple of problems with motorcycles.

During our third and final month at the academy, a riot occurred at the maximum-security section of one of our state prisons in Concord. It started with a hunger strike and developed to where a number of prisoners had taken a couple of guards as hostages and had taken over the exercise yard, threatening all sorts of violence. Our. commissioner, General Whitney, decided it might be a good experience for our academy class if they responded to the ongoing riot.

As a result, we were given a one hour crash course on a "Flying V" formation, a technique used when attempting to quell a riot. We were told that if anyone of us should go down, not to stop and assist but to step over the person and keep on going. Rifles were then issued but without ammunition as we were not yet fully certified as police officers. We were put on a bus, compliments of the U.S. Army at Fort Devins, and transported to the maximum-security section of the prison in Concord. As the bus arrived at the state police barracks, directly across the street, we were greeted by news reporters and television camera people. Prisoners who were still confined to their cells were screaming and banging their metal cups against the window bars. It was an eerie sight.

We lined up in formation with our empty rifles and, headed by one armed trooper, marched toward the massive swinging doors which led across the exercise yard where the two guards were being held hostage. All

50 magazines of our empty rifles snapped shut in unison and a trooper using a bullhorn announced that this was the prisoners' last chance to surrender. By then I was thinking that my old cement mixer looked pretty good. But all the convicts were aware of what state troopers thought of convicted felons and how they would react to their hostage taking. They wisely decided that enough was enough and gave up. I can assure you, all trainees including myself, slept well that night.

Graduation from the Massachusetts State Police Academy was quite an occasion. The week before, we started to prepare for it, marching and conducting exercises that would impress our audience and assure them they were receiving their tax dollars worth. Each trainee was given a brief exit interview by our academy commandant and all except the two previously mentioned casualties would graduate. I was of the distinct impression that our commandant wasn't too impressed with me. I was 23 years of age and looked a lot younger. He was probably more impressed with the macho type. I had scored above 90 in every test given and never in my three months at the academy had I received one critical remark from my instructors. So I was quite disappointed when I learned I was judged by the commandant to have graduated next to last. But I had graduated. It was pretty obvious to me anyway, that our commandant was of the opinion that former Marines and paratroopers would make the best police officers. This was not especially true as the rest of us, mostly Korean veterans, proved to be very capable as well. To me at least, discipline is a very important aspect in law enforcement, but without drive and determination, its value can be lessened. In fact 90% of police work is just plain common sense. We were sworn in as state troopers by the then Governor and later to become the U.S. Secretary of State, Christian A. Hurter and given three days off before reporting to our new assignments. Audrey, had endured my three month ordeal with very little complaining and we thoroughly enjoyed our time off together.

EIGHT

Wednesday, November 3,1954, I reported to State Police Holden, head-quarters for Troop C and subsequently to the Charlton City Barracks. Chariton City is about seven miles from the Connecticut state line. All new rookies were, at that time anyway, stationed quite far from their residences to undergo a six-month probation period before being transferred to another barracks. Although there was no formal FTO (Field Training Officer) at the time, I would ride with experienced troopers most of the time. As I got my feet wet, so to speak I was assigned to daytime patrols alone. The Charlton City barracks had about twelve troopers assigned there, including a sergeant and a corporal.

My new Sergeant tried to give off the image of a real tough boss but I found him to be a solid guy who had the respect of all his people. He took no guff from his superiors at Troop C Headquarters in Holden. In fact I personally remember one occasion when he called his lieutenant at Holden and complained when he thought one of his officers had been wrongly accused of something. When he didn't get the answer he wanted, he actually hung up on the lieutenant. The lieutenant called back offering that maybe they had been disconnected. Our sergeant replied, "No Lieutenant, I intentionally hung up on you." And hung up the phone again. Unheard of in those days. The man certainly had balls and he was a good cook too. I can recall enjoying many a good roast beef when our civilian cook was off duty.

At that time we worked an 89-hour week. Yes folks, I said 89 hours a week and overtime wasn't even in our vocabulary. We had two days off out of every eight. That included sleep of course if you were ever lucky to get any that is. My week started when I reported for duty at 10:00 AM as I lived 90 miles from the Charlton City barracks and was given two hours travel time. Upon reporting for duly I was expected to wash all available cruisers, usually two or three, or take a cruiser to our Holden headquarters for service and while there, do a patrol until the vehicle was ready. I would then return to Charlton City for our evening meal. After dinner I was assigned to an eight-hour patrol, routinely scheduled from 6:00 PM to 2:00 AM or 7:00 PM to 3:00 AM. At that time Chariton City covered the main artery from Massachusetts to Connecticut and New York City. In fact it really included access to the rest of The United States. Consequently, we had very heavy traffic activity and covered a lot of automobile accidents. Being short-handed it was not uncommon to stay out beyond the eight-hour patrol or get called out sometime during the remaining early hours of the morning. If we did make it through the early morning hours, usually we had District Court or Superior Court which required us to "rise and shine" by 7:00 AM.

On the second day of our tour, a trooper was assigned to a 1:00 PM to 2:00 AM patrol or a 10:00 AM to 8:00 PM patrol with a two hour break and then a night watch on the desk from 10:00 pm to 8:00 am, after which the sergeant or corporal took over.

I was lucky when starting my time off Audrey was still working for the telephone company and I was able to grab three or four hours of sleep before picking her up at work. So that was the life of a uniformed state trooper assigned to a barracks in Massachusetts. At that time, if a trooper actually lived in the area to which he was assigned and was caught stopping at home too many times, he would be transferred to another barracks some distance away. There was no union and we were not covered by Civil Service. Troopers were required to reenlist every two years.

Holiday time off was allotted by seniority naturally and although I was able to spend the Thanksgiving of 1954 with Audrey and both our folks, I had the duty at Charlton City that following Christmas. I had always enjoyed that particular season and now once again I had to work. In fact the barracks had been stripped and we were down to three troopers, two of us "rookies." But motor vehicle enforcement at Christmas time was limited to warnings only and fortunately there were very few accidents then. (See? Cops do have a heart occasionally.) Watching families motor along together with a car stuffed full of Christmas presents, off to celebrate the season with relatives or friends was for me a very lonesome experience. Having missed a Christmas at home at boot camp plus a couple of others during my military career, I felt rather depressed. I had thought all that was behind me. Wrong again "'Lonesome George."

At this point, let me explain the "Lonesome George" thing. It seemed like every trooper had a nickname, at least in my era. I'm not quite sure exactly why I was dubbed "Lonesome George." It may have been attributed to the fact that with my individual personality, I might have appeared to my coworkers as somewhat aloof. I personally would prefer the adjective "private" be considered but then again some would say that all New Englanders come across to others in the United States as aloof. Regardless, the nickname "Lonesome George" stuck with me and even today when I talk to anyone on the job with me who was a trooper will address me as "Lonesome."

While I was assigned to the Charlton City Barracks, I caught my first criminal case. During the winter, two teenagers had broken into one of the cottages around a lake in Southbridge. Finding no money or anything else of value, they did considerable damage to the interior of the cottage and must have worked up a real appetite in doing so as they opened up and ate whatever canned goods they could find, causing quite a mess. Through investigation, I came up with two strong suspects who were brought to the Southbridge Police Department for questioning. Of course, when initially questioned, both denied the burglary. We then questioned each separately in adjacent rooms and the first suspect again denied any implication. He was taken to a holding cell while the second suspect remained in the adjacent interview room. An officer on the other side of the wall banged heavily on the wall while another yelled, "Ouch! Ouch! Okay. I'll tell you." The officer with the second suspect asked him if he had heard that coming from his friend and the first suspect readily admitted that he and his companion had committed the burglary. After he related sufficient particulars to convince us that he was not lying to us, both were charged with Breaking and Entering and incarcerated.

Of course, both teenagers pleaded not guilty when arraigned at Southbridge District Court and both were represented by an attorney who before trial, asked to read my report of investigation. I was about to decline his request when a senior trooper accompanying me said, "He's okay. Give it to him," I reluctantly did so and we lost our case. I realized that the attorney was only doing his job but although I had no proof, I always suspected there had been a "good old boy" relationship between the attorney and the trooper and that was the last time I ever trusted a defense attorney. This was a long time prior to the Jenks Act which entitles a defendant in a federal prosecution case access to potentially incriminating evidence followed by our disclosure laws which now allow the defendant access to such material before trial. So under the criteria which exists today, the attorney would have had access to my report anyway. But I still had to author a memorandum to my superiors as to why we lost our case, as was the policy at that time. Of course I couldn't state what I thought the real reason was as to do so would have violated the "thin blue line" law that we all adhered to. That all has pretty much disappeared in law enforcement and maybe in some cases just as well but I think at the expense of the camaraderie we used to enjoy in our profession.

Both the food and our cook at Charlton City were good. In fact too good. Her strawberry shortcake with whipped cream seemed to be her favorite desert and between her cuisine and the Publix House, I was developing a weight problem. The Publix House, part of Surbridge Village, an attraction to tourists that displayed early life in New England, was a Class A restaurant and was located in our sector. Prior to my arrival at Charlton City, information had been received from a reliable informant that on a certain night, an armed robbery was being planned there and we responded with two troopers. Since they did not wish to alarm customers, the troopers took up positions at the rear of the restaurant. After they were in position for some time, two men entered the restaurant, robbed the cashier at gunpoint seizing a substantial amount of cash and fled out the back door only to be greeted by my colleagues. They were apprehended and charged with felony Armed Robbery and the money recovered.

Having witnessed all this, the manager of the Publix House appeared at the barracks the next day and pleaded with our sergeant to have our patrols periodically check the restaurant and in fact, without charge, feel free to sample the restaurant's attractive fare to their hearts' desire. Probably very inexpensive insurance for the Publix House. So after completing a night's patrol and nibbling on lobster Newberg, prime rib and other rich foods, I started to complain that the dry cleaner was shrinking my uniforms. So fighting "the battle of the bulge" I decided to knock off the extra weight and believe me, it wasn't easy passing up all that good stuff for eating cottage cheese on my late night snacks. But personal pride won and I dropped the extra 15 pounds I had gained.

Have you ever had the occasion to spend the night in a town dump? I did and if at all possible, I strongly suggest you avoid it. It happened while I was stationed at the Charlton City Barracks. The Auburn police reported that a burglary had occurred at H.P. Hood, a major milk company in New England, sometime during the previous night. The company's large safe containing several thousand dollars had been stolen. It was located the next morning in, of all places, the town dump. Apparently the burglars were unable to crack the safe and didn't have the right equipment to blow it up so they removed the safe, placed it in a truck and hauled it off to Auburn's town dump where they could later open it and remove the cash. Why would they do that? Well don't forget, we do not exactly deal with rocket scientists you know. For some reason we seem to give the criminal element in our society credit for a lot more intelligence than they deserve.

Anyway, a plan was devised to stake out this safe in the town dump and wait for the bad guys to return and attempt to open it. Since Auburn PD's resources were rather limited, they asked for state police assistance. My partner and I won the assignment and about 10:00 PM, along with two Auburn PD officers and their Chief, we crawled into the bushes near where the safe had been dumped. The chief was no help at all as he was so inebriated all we could hear during the night was his snoring. It was a hot New England summer night and you can imagine the odor reeking from that dump. Although I had covered myself with bug repellant, the mosquitoes were still driving me nuts. In those days we were only issued woolen uniforms with long sleeve shirts. Once again, I wondered if I had chosen the right occupation.

At one pointing time, lying there in the bushes, I spotted two beady eyes staring at me from about 15 feet away. A quick flash of my light revealed a rat which I swear was as big as a house cat, looking at me. I was hoping I wouldn't have to shoot the dammed thing but it finally became disinterested and disappeared.

By daybreak we were all hoping that the burglars would show up to open their prize and they did. But unfortunately we had a communication problem. Somebody forgot to tell the Auburn officer on routine patrol about our little stakeout and he spotted three men in a truck driving on a road leading to the dump. To the officer, they appeared suspicious at that hour and he stopped them. They never made it to our stakeout. However they did have burglary tools in their possession which was a felony in Massachusetts and their fingerprints were all over the safe. Once again justice prevailed and H.P. Hood was delighted.

NINE

After completing my six-month probationary period, I was transferred to the Grafton Barracks, still in Troop C and about 20 miles closer to our home in Holbrook. Having been exposed to a lot of experience in traffic enforcement, I got my second break as the Grafton Barracks had one of the heaviest criminal caseloads in the Commonwealth of Massachusetts. I'm not sure just why as we were some distance from Boston and its crime problems, but our sector did include some 18 small towns. Most of these had only a two or three officer department and they as well as their citizens relied heavily on state troopers for assistance.

The Grafton barracks had the same hours and patrol schedules as all other barracks and without the pressure of being on probation, I really started to focus on my new chosen profession. In fact two weeks after being transferred to Grafton, I caught my first investigation of a fatal accident. Three teenagers in a brand new Oldsmobile owned by the driver's dad, slammed into the rear end of a furniture truck on Route 146 in Millbury, killing the driver and seriously injuring the two other passengers. Although I had a little help with the traffic from two other troopers, they were soon called elsewhere and I had to deal with the whole scene alone including the filing of a prosecution case at Worcester District Court. At that time, state troopers prosecuted their own cases in the District Courts. This included not only testifying but presenting the state's witnesses and cross-examining the defendant and his or her witnesses. This caused much consternation to defense attorneys who often objected but were always overruled by the sitting judge. It also required me to spend a lot of my own time in law libraries, preparing my case. If it was a felony and the case was bound over for Grand Jury and an indictment obtained, as was usually the case, an Assistant District Attorney would try the case in Superior Court.

Our sector at Grafton also included two state hospitals that housed people with severe mental problems, some suicidal. Occasionally a patient would escape, or maybe a better choice of words, wander off, and we would retrieve the poor soul and return him or her to the appropriate facility. This task was not always an easy one because when a patient was picked up, you never really knew what you had. Some could be violent and potentially dangerous. As I previously mentioned, a backup was almost never available and I usually found myself working alone.

I can recall on one occasion, I was off duty in civilian clothes late at night and in the middle of nowhere in my own car when I spotted a middle-aged man walking along a country road. There was no indication that he was walking away from a disabled vehicle and although the weather was cold, he didn't have any coat or hat on. Now it has always been my personal policy not to make an arrest unless I was in uniform or had a backup, unless of course a citizen's life was in immediate danger. But this guy, out here in the boondocks was either going to get run over or scare the daylights out of some citizen. I identified myself and after our initial conversation, I realized he had mental problems. He had admitted being a patient at the Westborough State Hospital so I cuffed him, put him in my personal vehicle and transported him back to that facility. As was the policy then, a patient could not be readmitted without an interview with the psychiatrist on duty. The psychiatrist on duty at 2:00 AM was a middle-aged man with straggly hair and wearing a beard which was long before beards were stylish. He called the patient into his office and I remained outside. Not wanting to get involved, in the interview process I stood some distance away but I couldn't help overhearing some of the questions that sounded to me a little weird. After several moments, the patient got up, walked over to me and said, "Hey, you think I'm crazy? This guy's crazier than I am."

On another occasion, I was doubled with another trooper patrolling Route 20 in Shrewsbury. It was late at night and there was a full moon. We observed a man in the middle of the road on his hands and knees crawling along the white line that separates the eastbound traffic from the westbound. We stopped our cruiser, approached him and inquired as to what he was doing. He said, "I'm rolling up the white line. It doesn't belong here." Further inquiry revealed him to be a resident of the Worcester State Hospital and we deposited him back there.

In my tour of duty at the Grafton Barracks, I only caught one rape case. If you could call it a rape case, that is. The alleged rape was reported by a middle-aged lady, a resident of the Westborough State Hospital. It seemed that she and her male companion were sunning themselves on the shore of a lake that was part of the hospital complex. They became romantically

31

involved. She claimed he attempted to rape her, called the Westborough Police department and both were both picked up for questioning before calling the Grafton Barracks for assistance. This was before the days of female police officers and the state police employed policewomen, also sworn officers, who assisted in the investigation of juvenile cases and all sex crimes. I was assigned a young policewoman with only two weeks on the job.

We arrived at the Westborough Police Station and I began to question the male and female separately. The female still alleged rape and the male insisted that the female wanted him to get down on her. He refused and she called the police claiming he tried to rape her. This was of course, a "one on one" situation with no physical evidence being present. The Clerk of Court wisely declined to issue a complaint and both were released from custody and returned to the Westborough State Hospital.

My policewoman, being a rookie, quietly took all this in without comment. But on our drive back to the Grafton Barracks she asked me what the man meant when he said that the lady wanted him to get down on her. I immediately turned bright red, struggling to think of an appropriate but dignified answer and finally came up with "I think it's referred to in our criminal statutes as an unnatural act." I often wondered if, after getting a little more experience, she ever reflected back on our conversation. Incidentally, she turned out to be a very capable and successful officer.

As previously mentioned, everyone in our academy class survived motorcycle training with the exception of the trainee who went through the barn door. In my tenure at Grafton, other than parades and escort duties, troopers were only assigned motorcycles if the sector was adequately covered by radio equipped cruisers and then only patrolled rural areas during the last four hours of their three-day tour. At the time, more officers had been injured on motorcycles than by any other facet of our work.

Incidentally, two-way radios had been installed in motorcycles before my time but it seemed the radios had a low survival rate. When a trooper had been assigned a radio-equipped motorcycle, his bike went over a curb or two, thereby causing the radio to malfunction. Of course the trooper could not then respond to a radio call one hour before starting his time off. Management gave up and motorcycles were no longer equipped with two-way radios.

Riding on three inches of rubber on a motorcycle never really appealed to me that much and the only speeder I ever chased on a motorcycle was during a rainstorm and the guy practically ran over me.

Then there was the time I had one catch on fire and that really made me leery of them. It happened on Lyman Street in Westborough, ironically directly in front of a house lot later to become the location of our first home. I had just come off Route 9, a major thoroughfare, traveling only about 35 MPH when I happened to look down and saw a fire had started under my seat. Apparently some electrical wires had short-circuited and there was a nice little fire burning under me adjacent to the gasoline tank. Immediately I leaned that sucker over and hopped off to await a neighbor's call to the fire department. After that, I wasn't exactly thrilled when assigned a motorcycle but Harley Davidson wasn't through with me yet.

While still at the Grafton Barracks, I was assigned as the lone police escort for the Adlai Stevenson motorcade. Stevenson was running on the Democratic ticket for President against Dwight Eisenhower and I was to meet the motorcade in Worcester and escort it down Route 140, past the Grafton Barracks to Milford where there would be a political rally late that afternoon. The rally was being held in the city's graveyard of all places.

Everything had gone along nicely until we arrived at the graveyard where a crowd had gathered. As we approached a key monument, the mechanism regulating my speed control froze, sending my bike up a small knoll narrowly missing five or six gravestones before I could get the dammed thing stopped. I'm sure there were several Secret Service Agents glaring at me wondering, "what the hell is that trooper doing?"

The political rally ended without further interruption but my motorcycle was still inoperative and the motorcade was forced to depart the area on its own. It was very late in the day before I got the bike operational and finally I started back toward the Grafton Barracks. As I headed up Route 140 passing through the small town of Upton, someone stepped out in front of me, flagging me down. I stopped and he pointed to a car that had run off the road striking a tree. My helpful citizen advised me that the driver of the vehicle was still in the driver's seat, apparently uninjured but dead drunk.

Swell! Here I was in the middle of nowhere, pitch dark without a flashlight or a radio with a drunk I could ill afford to leave lest he wander out on the road and cause yet another accident. I was well aware that I probably couldn't get help from the Upton Police Department which at the time had only one part-time officer who was probably home enjoying his evening meal.

I dragged the driver out of his vehicle, handcuffed him and finally flagged down a motorist who would pass the Grafton Barracks on Route 140. I instructed him to stop there and inform the duty trooper of my dilemma. It was about an hour before a cruiser came to my rescue, relieved me of my prisoner and we all headed back to the barracks for a very late meal.

Now I am well aware that many people even today, enjoy riding motorcycles and I respect that. But today, if you should happen to peek in the garage at my home, I sincerely doubt you would find a motorcycle parked next to our Cadillac.

Although we had a lot of criminal activity at Grafton, there was still plenty of traffic enforcement and in all my years chasing speeders, the only time I refused to give an off duty officer "professional courtesy" if you will, was when I was stationed at Grafton. One weekend night, one of my class-mates, Mike Rizzo and I were patrolling together. We had picked up a vehicle traveling east on Route 9 in Northborough with four occupants. I clocked it at 115 MPH and it was almost to Framingham about eight miles away before we finally got it stopped. While I was too busy driving to be scared, Rizzo's face, he being of Italian extraction with fairly dark complexion, was pure white. The vehicle had out-of state license plates and was driven by an individual who claimed he was a professional boxer. Although he was reasonably sober, the other occupants weren't. One of the passengers sitting in the rear seat, got out of the car and identified himself as an off duty officer with NYPD. He asked us for professional courtesy and I declined. He became quite upset, advising us that if we were ever stopped in New York City we would have been given professional courtesy. I replied, "Mister, if I ever got caught in New York City driving 115 MPH, I wouldn't have the balls to identify myself as a police officer and ask for professional courtesy." He mumbled something and got back in the car.

In Massachusetts all individuals accused of a crime, be it a misdemeanor or a felony, are arraigned in a District Court. All District Court judges are appointed by the Governor. In many other states a judge may be elected by the people. The process can be argued either way as an elected judge can allow his or her judgment to be effected by an upcoming election. However, a judge appointed for life can also be rather uncontrollable, but personally I have never seen that occur.

At any rate, District Court judges dispose of all cases, misdemeanors decided at that hearing and felony cases bound over for the Grand Jury if the judge decides that probable cause exists.

As a trooper, I spent a lot of time in District Courts, presenting my evidence, cross-examining the defendant and his or her witnesses. Usually the setting in a courtroom is rather solemn but occasionally humor can creep in.

In Worcester District Court, Judges Riley and Allen sat alternately during the week. Judge Riley was quite elderly and Judge Allen about 20 years younger. Each was considered by police officers to be a "cop's judge," that is, tough but fair.

I remember Judge Riley having a rather prominent proboscis. After the prosecution and defense concluded, Judge Riley would reach for the complaint and decide whether the defendant was guilty or not guilty of a misdemeanor, or in the case of a felony, the defendant would be bound over for the Grand Jury. He would note this on the complaint but before doing so, if his decision had been in favor of the state, he would grab that big nose of his for a few seconds. The arresting officer was always relieved to see Judge Riley grab that honker before writing his decision on the complaint.

District Court routinely started at 9:00 AM with the disposing of the previous night's drunk tank first. These cases always appeared first on the court's docket. I can recall one morning I was awaiting my case to be called by Judge Riley's clerk and a Worcester police officer had, the night before, arrested a rather beat up middle age female on Front Street, not the best part of town. She'd had numerous previous arrests for intoxication and was well known to Worcester PD. The officer routinely testified that her faculties had been greatly impaired and that he smelled a strong odor of alcohol about her person. For some reason he then added, "And Your Honor, the defendant made some derogatory remarks about the court." Judge Riley then looked up at the officer and said, "What kind of remarks, officer?" The officer replied that he didn't think these remarks would be appropriate to repeat in a courtroom. Judge Riley then said, "Officer, I am directing you to answer my question. What did the defendant say?" The officer, wishing he hadn't added this to his testimony said, "Well, when I picked her up in my cruiser, Your Honor, she asked who the judge would be in the morning. When I answered her question she said, "Well, f.... that old bastard." Judge Riley then grinned and replied, "Humm. She must have thought that Judge Allen was sitting this morning." Everyone in the courtroom roared.

Now, many troopers, I found, had favorite spots where they could find frequent motor vehicle violations at high-risk accident locations and I was no exception. My favorite spot was a location known by my coworkers as "George's Hill." It was located on Route 20 in Shrewsbury where heading east, motorists came down a long hill and then headed up on a three lane road with a solid white line indicating a no passing zone heading east. There was a passing zone heading west and motorists heading east too often crossed over the solid white line blindly heading up the hill and we had many a head-on collision there. Very dangerous! So many days while on patrol I tried to spend a little time there observing traffic and hoping to save a life or two.

One afternoon I was standing beside my cruiser at the top of "George's Hill." I happened to look down at the railroad tracks below and as they say, "lo and behold," I saw two youngsters trudging along the tracks. One was a boy about five years old and a little girl younger than he. "Something is wrong here," I said to myself. I jumped over the guardrail and somehow managed to climb down the hill, scoop them both up and get them back to my cruiser. The boy said, "We were just taking a walk," and I cautioned them as to the danger of a train running over them. I put them in my cruiser to take them home but neither had any idea of where they lived and we had not received any report of missing children. I thought maybe they were visiting with their dad who had a business somewhere on Route 20 and had wandered off unnoticed. So I asked the little boy, "What does your dad do?" He replied, "Well, he yells a lot." Big help, huh? Eventually I drove them through the neighborhood and they finally recognized their home. I turned them over to their mother who appeared somewhat worried. She promised she would keep a closer eye on them.

Now, "George's Hill" also produced an embarrassment to me. One day I was standing there observing traffic when a Pontiac sedan came down the hill heading east and crossing over the solid white line passed another vehicle going up the hill in the same direction. I stepped out holding up my hand and the sole occupant immediately stopped. I informed him of the violation and he could only produce a valid Massachusetts driver's license. He was unable to come up with the vehicle's registration and I had to radio it in. The driver's license read James Pearsall of Newtonville, Massachusetts, my hometown, of course. Records revealed he was the valid owner of the car and I gave him a citation. He was very polite under the circumstances and not being a baseball fan, I gave the matter no further thought. But when I got back to the Grafton Barracks for the evening meal, did I ever catch it from my fellow troopers. It seemed I had stopped the famous Jimmy Pearsall, a Boston Red Sox star who was considered a superb athlete, but who also had a reputation for having a temper, which the news media openly noted. Oh well, so much for celebrities. He had still been a danger to traffic coming the other way.

While stationed in Grafton I can recall responding to a situation which still haunts me even today. It was about 10:00 PM and Trooper Paul Kane and I were patrolling in the Blackstone Valley area of our district. We received a radio call that there was a fire raging at a multiple story dwelling in Uxbridge. We happened to be in Uxbridge and it took us only a few minutes to arrive. Indeed there was an inferno raging in a rather shabby wooden structure. As we arrived, neighbors indicated that a youngster had been rescued from the home and was still unconscious. They also indicated there was a second child still inside on the second floor. Kane immediately began to work on the first boy still unconscious and I went to where somebody had placed a ladder outside a second story bedroom window. I climbed up the ladder but the flames and smoke were just pouring out of that bedroom window. The fire department had not yet arrived but I could hear the sirens in the distance. I made several attempts to enter through the window but with the flames and smoke I couldn't breathe. After several attempts to get

36

through the window, I felt someone shaking my ladder. I looked down to see a fireman there with a mask on. He motioned me to come down and he went up through the window. Eventually he came down with a second unconscious boy in his arms. The kid was so black I couldn't even determine what race he was. I started to give him mouth to mouth even though his throat was just filled with soot. I dug out as much as I could and continued my attempt to get him breathing again. Minutes later an ambulance arrived and both youngsters were taken to the nearest hospital. The boy Trooper Kane had worked on survived but the boy I had worked on did not. I often pondered if I had gotten into that bedroom earlier myself whether the boy's life might have been saved.

Many civilians, most of them youngsters, being fascinated by cop movies and television shows, have asked me over the years if I had ever shot anyone or had I been shot at. Actually most of us in this profession have all enjoyed the "Dirty Harry" movies as we watched Clint Eastwood get away with stuff that if pulled, we would get fired in a New York minute.

At any rate, there was an incident where I almost bought the farm. I had been temporarily assigned to the Brookfield Barracks which was supposed to be a rather quiet sector, mostly rural. Corporal Joe Cooney and I were doing a patrol one evening when we received a radio transmission that someone was shooting at motorists passing by a residence. The location was furnished and when Joe and I arrived at the scene, we found a modest dwelling set back from the roadway about 75 yards. We observed a teenage male standing outside the dwelling's front door firing what appeared to be a 22-caliber rifle, randomly toward the street. Joe and I leaped from the cruiser into the tall grass surrounding the dwelling. Of course, it was pitch black and I held out my flashlight at arm's length in case I was to be a target, hoping that whoever was shooting would aim at my flashlight. That move may have saved me a headshot because this kid fired a round at me missing my right ear by about three inches. I could actually hear the round whizzing by and believe me it's a sound one never forgets. I yelled, "State Police. Drop the gun or you're dead." He hesitated and I was able to talk him out of the weapon which he finally put down. His mother stood by wringing her hands and pleading with us. "I tried to stop him but he just wouldn't listen." We could have charged the kid with Aggravated Assault on a Police Officer, a felony but softy here just charged him with Illegal Discharge of a Firearm, hoping eventually the kid might get his head screwed on straight and end up a law-abiding citizen. But then statistics show there is a very dim success rate with criminal rehabilitation and it has always been my opinion that leopards never seem to change their spots. You will find that most law enforcement officers tend to be rather cynical and with good reason. One goes to church on Sunday, listens and prays but then returns back to the real world on the street where once again, the officer struggles with the criminal element and those who would harm others and their property.

And speaking of the potential for getting shot, I learned a very valuable lesson in the early years of my career in law enforcement. It's that frivolous or cursory searches can kill you. One night, Trooper Dick Barry and I spotted two young males hitchhiking toward New York City. For some reason, they just didn't look right to us and we asked them for their IDs. We questioned them further and they alleged they had been in Boston that day but couldn't explain just where or why. A cursory search revealed one had a six-inch knife secreted on his person. We took them both back to the Grafton Barracks for further questioning. A more thorough search at the barracks revealed the other suspect had a loaded 45 caliber automatic pistol hidden in his crotch, no less. Dick and I had missed it in our initial cursory search. Before the sun rose the following morning, they admitted to committing 16 burglaries in central Massachusetts. The one with the knife had no previous record and received probation. The other one with the gun had a previous record and received five years in the penitentiary. So like I said, there's no such thing as a cursory search. It can kill you.

While I was stationed at Grafton, the maximum-security prison at Concord had another problem. Somehow a prisoner managed to escape, steal a Ford Country Squire station wagon which had been immediately reported stolen and had taken off for parts unknown. It was not known whether he was armed. The Grafton Barracks was stripped of all personnel except the desk officer and one trooper who was on patrol. That was me. All other troopers were directed to the Concord area to search for the escaped prisoner.

Shortly thereafter in Newton, city of my birthplace and about 20 miles from Concord, police reported that a Ford station wagon, answering the same description as our escapee's vehicle , was traveling at high speed on Route 9 in Newton westbound, towards Southborough where I was. They said the vehicle was traveling so fast police were unable to get the license plate number. I thought ,"Wow! Here's my chance to make a good arrest." I took up a position at an intersection with a traffic light on Route 9.

About 15 minutes later, the suspect vehicle flew through the intersection at a very high speed and I was on his tail. Now police policy has always been that when making a traffic stop, the officer should stop his vehicle behind the motorist's vehicle rather than in front of it. This protects the officer's safety as well as the motorist's.   But the clown driving this car saw my strobe lights and heard my siren. He immediately slammed on his brakes, forcing me to go beyond his vehicle before I could safely stop. It was a downhill area and pitch black. Not very good. I will never forget that walk back to the suspect's car with its headlights shining on me and not knowing if he was armed or not. But when I finally got to the vehicle without getting shot, I found I didn't have the Concord escapee in a stolen car. All I had was a dammed drunk who reeked of alcohol. I arrested him, cuffed him and placed him in the right rear seat of cruiser. He became so violent, he caused such severe damage to the interior of my cruiser. I used photographs of the damage in District Court concerning the charge of Driving Under The Influence of Alcohol. In spite of my testimony and the photographs, he was still found not guilty.

I was stunned as the sitting judge was respected by all in uniform and considered tough but fair. When court recessed, the judge requested I join him in his chambers. He advised me that his verdict of not guilty in no way was due to my lack of investigation or poor presentation of the evidence. He said that indeed, I had done an excellent job but that the defendant had been a classmate of his in law school many years ago. I thought it rather decent of him to share this with me as he certainly didn't have to. But that slogan over the doorway of many courtrooms in this country that says "Equal Justice for All" isn't always very accurate.

<u>TEN</u>

After about two years at the Grafton Barracks, I really got a break. I was reassigned to our Criminal Information Bureau in Boston. The reason it was a big break was because I no longer had to live like a "tin soldier" in a barracks but was allowed to work out of my home. Audrey was delighted too. Our Criminal Information Bureau or CIB was really our version of a vice squad. I was assigned to work undercover with a partner collecting intelligence information concerning bookmakers. We would spend each day in a different major city, frequenting bars that bookmakers operated out of, observe their modus operandi and our information would be subsequently reported to The Chief of Police in that particular community. After our information had been reported three or four times and the chief either did not respond or no correction action was taken, other troopers working undercover would place bets with the bookmaker and he would be subsequently arrested and prosecuted. This did not exactly enhance our image with local authorities but may I point out that at least in Massachusetts bookmakers had a direct relationship with organized crime people and couldn't operate without their blessing. In fact in one major city, while working undercover gathering intelligence information, I actually observed a local police cruiser parked in back of a bar and two local officers inside placing bets. Enough about police corruption.

Adjusting to my undercover work in CIB wasn't easy at first. To frequent eight or ten bars every day to collect our required information, one had to drink beer. Now don't misunderstand me. I like beer. But eight or ten beers during the course of a day was taking its toll on me and I would get home at night wondering how in the world I would be able to continually cope with this routine. I finally figured out a way. When I entered a bar, I would order a draft beer, take a sip or two and if no bookmaker was observed. I would go to the men's room for a few minutes and then slip out the door, unnoticed. Even when I observed a bookmaker taking bets, I would limit my sips. And it worked. I would arrive home feeling normal once again. Of course the job required night work too when the dog tracks were open as we had to pursue bookmakers who booked dog bets as well as horse bets.

While I was assigned to our Vice Squad in Boston, we received a rather interesting request from the Commander of Troop C. in Holden for an undercover officer. Since I lived in Troop C's sector, I was given the assignment. This made me a little apprehensive as the Commander of Troop C had been the commandant of our State Police Academy when I had attended and I was mindful of my exit interview when he advised me I had ranked next to last in our graduating class. I reported to the Troop Commander and he related that the Troop C sector (central Massachusetts) had a problem with payoff's on pinball machines. It seemed that there had been several complaints that teenagers had been attracted to small establishments in the area who were illegally paying off teenagers for winning games at these pinball machines. The Troop Commander wanted me to establish where these pinball machines were located in his sector so that the matter might be corrected through further enforcement.

It took me about two weeks to cover all the cities and towns where the pinball machines were located and indeed I observed several teenagers taking illegal payoffs. Having established the location of these establishments paying off on their pinball machines, I wrote a detailed report including a rather elaborate color map showing the locations. The Troop Commander seemed delighted with my results and commended me for a job well done. I left his office with a big smile on my face and probably feeling a bit smug as now my former Academy Commandant seemed to have a rather different opinion of that baby faced trainee he knew just a few years previous. It was, I confess, one of life's sweetest moments.

However, as in every other occupation, once a task is performed rather well, one is called upon to accept an equally challenging one and once again we heard from the Commander of Troop C. Through intelligence gathering, it had been learned that an individual known to be in the lower echelon of local organized crime had recently built a modest dwelling on a lake in Spencer, Massachusetts and many vehicles had been seen coming and going, bearing out-of-state license plates. A number of them were from New York State and gambling and other illegal activity was suspected. The Troop C Commander requested an undercover surveillance be conducted at the suspect's lake house to confirm intelligence information. He specifically requested my participation. So in the summer of 1959, my partner Trooper Bob Fountaine and I reported for assignment. The commander explained the situation to us and advised that all necessary expenses would be reimbursed.

After reconnoitering the suspect's lake house and surroundings, we entered a wooded area across the small lake with a view of the dwelling. Indeed, we did spot quite a few visitors with out-of-state plates, coming and going, a number of which were New York license plates. However our surveillance position had to change as Bob was being heavily harassed by mosquitoes. I had anticipated the problem and had brought along mosquito repellent but Bob had not and was miserable. So the following day, with some borrowed fishing equipment, we rented a canoe and were not only more comfortable but able to get a closer look at the lake house and in fact using binoculars rather discreetly, were able to record several license tags of suspected vehicles. We spent another day keeping the lake house under surveillance and with the information we had gathered and other intelligence, we had sufficient probable cause for a search warrant of the lake house. A raid plan with uniformed troopers was then fine tuned.

At a signal from us in the canoe, a team of troopers hit the font door and one trooper hit the back door. Now from my experience at least, the back door of a residential dwelling usually leads to a porch, a mudroom or even the kitchen, but not this house. Troopers found out differently here. It seemed that the back door led directly into the only bathroom in the house. When my classmate, Fran Carlson put his size 12 boot through the door forcing it open, he found a young lady sitting on the commode in a state of shock. Can you imagine sitting on a commode in the privacy of your own bathroom on a peaceful summer day overlooking a picturesque little lake when a six foot three 240-pound state trooper stomps through the door? Needless to say, she was in quite a disarray and Carlson, rather embarrassed, allowed her haul up her jeans before he proceeded further. Troopers were able to make several arrests and once again the Troop C Commander was a happy man.

ELEVEN

I had been chasing bookmakers and other suspects involved in vice type crimes for about a year when a vacancy appeared in our Narcotics Unit. Actually, it really wasn't big enough for a division in those days. It was only a unit with seven troopers to cover the whole state. A vacancy occurred in Troop C covering central Massachusetts and not only did the work appeal to me but by that time, Audrey and I had bought our first house in Westborough which was in Troop C's sector. So I put in for it and it was approved. My new office was in Holden, Troop C Headquarters and I was still able to live at home. Now my nickname "Lonesome George" was really appropriate because alone, I had to cover 38 cities and towns, only two of which had any sort of Narcotics Unit, Worcester PD and Fitchburg PD. The rest of these police departments, when faced with any type of drug investigation, depended on me. Consequently a 12 to 15 hour day was not all that unusual. But I was still living at home, at least when I was there.

When unformed troopers picked up someone with illegal drugs, I responded with a test kit I had developed which would initially identify amphetamines or "uppers," barbiturates or "downers" and heroin. We made many arrests and I had many long hours. (Audrey thought too damned many.) I can recall after one long arduous week she said to me, "We don't even have a chance to talk anymore. Tonight let's go to an open-air theater. I don't care what's playing. At least we can talk and plan our lives a little." I replied, "Sounds like a plan to me" and we loaded our two kids into the back of our car and headed for an open-air movie. We spent the entire evening talking and planning and returned home about 11:00 PM. As we pulled up to our house, there in the driveway sat three local police cruisers waiting with prisoners suspected of possessing illegal drugs. Audrey simply shook her head and put the kids to bed while I took care of business.

On another occasion, our doorbell rang at about 2:00 AM. I responded to find a Westborough police officer standing there with a suspect. I invited them into our living room for initial interrogation and to identify the drugs the suspect had on his person. Audrey hit the roof and told me under no circumstances would she put up with dope dealers in our living room. She was right of course and after that, I met all officers and their suspects at their station houses.

In those days, heroin was rather scarce in central Massachusetts and federal drug officials claimed that cocaine was merely a recreational drug and not addictive. Boy! How wrong can you be? But there was an exempt narcotic law in effect and addicts would simply sign a name, any name, and purchase cough medicine with codeine, a derivative of opium, to satisfy their habits. This became a serious problem and I spent many a day looking for exempt narcotics and forged prescriptions purchased by addicts. We made a lot of arrests. When I was sent for training at the Federal Bureau of Narcotics in Washington, D.C., now Drug Enforcement Agency, officials there said exempt narcotics were really not a problem. I argued bitterly but they just became irritated with me. Two or three years later, exempt narcotics were outlawed. One of the best "I told you so's" I ever enjoyed.

Working narcotic cases often involved surveillance and I spent many hours working a one person surveillance. I can assure you that a one person surveillance is not always that effective as a suspect can suddenly leave his vehicle, leaving you stuck in traffic or on the street walking. He can quickly jump into a vehicle and leave you standing there. One red light or other obstacle separating you and your suspect and your suspect can disappear. Any surveillance should have at least two undercover cars, each with a driver and a "leg man" and radio communication. I didn't have that luxury but occasionally got lucky.

I recall one case where a suspect was stealing prescriptions from a doctor and forging them to get Demerol. He was given six months in the Worcester House of Correction (county jail). In fact later, figuring I would make a better friend than enemy, he became one of my more reliable informants. One day after his release from jail, I needed some information and drove to his home. He was sitting in his back yard when I approached on foot. He took one look at me, jumped up and cried, "I didn't do it and I can prove it! I was in jail at the time and in fact you put me there." He was, I learned referring to a fire that had occurred in our home two months previous, causing damage by a butane gas tank, sufficient enough to leave the house unoccupied for four months. I replied, " Charlie, I know you didn't do it. The gas man did it." Of course, that was the case.

We also had a serious problem at the time with truckers using amphetamine pills or "bennies" to keep awake while driving long distances which was of course extremely dangerous. Mostly it involved "gypsy" truckers who owned their own tractors and would drive a company's trailer full of freight across the country, being paid by the mile. They were very underpaid, hard working men trying desperately to support their families but were in fact a hazard to other motorists. Most of these truckers seemed to reside in our southern states for some reason. The words "Teamsters Union" were not in their vocabulary. I can recall one driver who had driven from Florida en route to Boston nonstop, a distance of about 1,700 miles. His eyes were so dilated they looked like the bottom of Coke bottles. I asked him if he knew where he was and he replied, "Sure, "I'm just outside of Chicago." Chicago is about 1,500 miles from Boston.

From time to time, inspectors of the Interstate Commerce Commission, now the Department of Transportation, held safety inspections at the Massachusetts-Connecticut state line. To stop truckers in a safe manner they used uniformed state troopers and I often joined them looking for truckers using illegal amphetamines and found many were. We averaged about five or six arrests during the course of one day. They were charged with Illegal Possession of Dangerous Drugs, a misdemeanor, incarcerated overnight as they never were able to make bail, and arraigned the following morning. Many of them disclosed where they had purchased the drugs illegally, usually some diner in one of our southern states. When they did, the District Court Judge, with my encouragement, lowered the fine.

I remember one situation where a trucker arrested by a uniformed trooper for illegal possession of amphetamines, appeared in District Court the following morning and the regular judge was on vacation. The visiting judge had apparently no experience with truckers illegally using amphetamines and decided to make an example of him. He gave the trucker 30 days in the county jail. The uniformed trooper and I were appalled. We knew the company owning the trailer which was refrigerated and full of food, would have to retrieve the trailer and the trucker would probably be fired. In addition, the trucker's tractor would be towed away at his expense. We felt that while the trucker had been a danger to other motorists, the penalty had been way to severe and it bothered us. So when the regular judge returned from vacation about five or six days later, I met him in his chambers and explained what had happened. He immediately took action, causing the trucker to be released from jail. I often wondered whether that trucker is still scratching his head as to why he had suddenly been released before completing his sentence.

In another situation, I received information that someone was peddling drugs out of a bar in Worcester, so I began working undercover nights. It was one real bad place. It looked like every thief, burglar and pervert congregated in this joint. In fact, it was so bad I asked Worcester detectives why they didn't shut the place down. Their response was, "If we shut it down they will scatter all over the city and we'll never be able to find them when we want them. If we leave that bar open, when we're looking for a wanted person or suspect, it's a one stopper for us because chances are we'll find him there." It made sense to me anyway.

Once again, I asked for an undercover backup trooper and once again was told we were short handed and if I got in trouble just "drop a dime." I envisioned being in an alley somewhere in Worcester in the middle of the night facing a dope dealer and armed only with my 32-caliber Beretta undercover weapon stuffed in my jeans and signaling him a football timeout hand signal, telling him I had to drop a dime. Not really! But a close civilian friend of mine volunteered to watch my back. He wouldn't be armed but I reluctantly agreed. The first night I really couldn't get much conversation out of my friend other than "I don't believe this. I really can't believe it!"

Within a couple of weeks, I finally got close to a dope dealer who constantly complained about the state police "Gestapo" (uniformed troopers) harassing him on the road, looking for his dope. Of course I readily bad-mouthed the troopers, hoping my guys wouldn't find any dope and lock this scumbag up for possession before I was able to make a couple of heroin buys from him and put him away for a few years.

Now it was the policy of our Uniformed Division to pull every trooper working special assignments, including those working undercover, off into uniformed patrol on major holiday weekends. The Fourth of July weekend had come up right after I had gotten real close to my dope dealer in the Worcester bar. I had left the bar at about 1:00 AM, grabbed a little sleep at the house and was to report for uniformed patrol duty on the Massachusetts Turnpike at Sturbridge at 11:00 AM. I decided to stop at Howard Johnson's Restaurant on the turnpike just east of the barracks for a quick cup of coffee. Naturally, I was in uniform and just as I was sliding off the bar stool, who walks in but my dope dealer. Of course I had shaved off a week's growth of beard and had cleaned up my act a little and the dope dealer was about 25 feet away from me but he still looked at me. My stomach flipped. It was a long three days for me before I found out whether or not he recognized me .But as I went back into that Worcester bar again working undercover, I was relieved to find out he had not. He had probably been hung over or high on something and eventually I was able to make a couple of heroin buys and put him away for the illegal sale of narcotics.

Another interesting case I had while assigned to our Narcotics Unit occurred when a state police sergeant assigned to our Holden Barracks, while riding a local bus from Milford to Holden, was approached by the bus driver stating that there was a certain female running heroin from New York City to Milford. Investigation showed her to be living with a pharmacist who worked in a drug store in Milford which I thought was interesting. The driver subsequently tipped me off as to when she was again to travel to New York City, apparently to buy more heroin. We were even able to get the street name of the New York City drug dealer. By surveillance, I put her on a Greyhound bus bound for New York City and coordinated with Federal Bureau of Narcotics (now DEA) who was to pick up the girl and trail her to her source, which they did. I was informed that she would be under continuous surveillance until she boarded another Greyhound bound for Worcester and I would be notified.

The following morning, I patiently waited but no phone call came. At about 5:00 AM, seeing me toss and turn all night, Audrey said that she was not getting any sleep either and suggested I just go and do my own thing. I dressed and met every Greyhound bus coming into Worcester from New York City. My good friend, Police Lieutenant Grace O'Dell was with me and about 9:00 AM that morning, our suspect arrived and headed directly to the ladies room at the terminal. I asked Grace to cover the situation and she observed our suspect shooting up at an adjacent stall. The suspect then boarded a bus to Milford. We tailed the bus and when she got off in Milford, we arrested her and took her to the Milford Police Station. Pointing to a separate room which afforded privacy I said, "Grace, search her and I mean really search her. Okay?" Grace replied, "Gotcha, Lonesome." They both returned shortly later and our prisoner looked a little flustered. She complained, "She can't do that!" I said, "Oh yes, she can." Grace had found a quantity of heroin plus the prisoner's works, a needle and syringe. She was incarcerated and further investigation revealed that her boyfriend pharmacist had been supplying her with narcotics stolen from his employer, a local drug store. He was also prosecuted and of course lost his job and his pharmacist's license.

I had another case in Fitchburg, a medium size city in central Massachusetts. My initial investigation revealed that a drugstore there was significantly short on its prescription drug inventory with respect to amphetamines, designated as a dangerous drug in Massachusetts. A young pharmacist, who we shall call Wilbur, seemed to be my only suspect. About a block away from the drugstore was a bar and coincidentally I had received information that someone there was peddling illegal drugs. The bar was being operated by a convicted felon, even though his name was not on the liquor license. The Fitchburg Chief of Police I learned, was about to shut the place down and I pleaded with him to leave the bar open a couple more weeks until I could ascertain the source of the illegal drugs. He reluctantly agreed and I went undercover there for several nights.

Now this place was a real "bucket of blood" and I mean tough. Again I pleaded for a backup and surprisingly. Sergeant John Regan joined me. John, a long time close friend and one of the most capable officers I ever had the privilege to work with, subsequently became the Chief of Detectives before his untimely death from cancer.

We knew we would need a good cover working in this "den of iniquity" and we decided to pose as long distance gypsy truck drivers. Through a good connection, I was able to borrow a "Jimmy Smoker" which is a GMC diesel tractor. I didn't need a trailer as just a tractor would suffice. John and I would roll up to that bar in the tractor, dressed suitably and were accepted as just a couple of truck drivers passing through. The first night, we went up to the bar, ordered a beer and within five minutes, somebody threw a guy through the plate glass window. John looked at me and said, "Lonesome? This is a tough f...... place." I replied, "John, that's what I've been trying to tell our captain."

But Regan was good. He took several orders for illegal weapons which he promised to deliver on our next trip "back north." So we were in. We were even able to convince the convicted felon running the place, as he bought us drinks at another bar nearby. I also managed to get the confidence of another criminal, burglar by trade, who continually bragged about how many "boxes" (safes) he had broken into and how much money he had stolen. I noticed he was still broke but of course I appeared impressed. To me, the problem with undercover work was watching my tongue. Associating with these scumbags required a lot of self-control but when there is the potential for danger, one comes up with a lot of B.S.

Actually, along with my ability to B.S. at least some of the criminal element, I had my appearance going for me. I did not seem to come across as your typical cop, let alone the prestigious state trooper. I was of medium height, medium build and I had what I considered an unimpressive appearance. Not a hell of a lot of self-esteem in that I know, but to the bad guys, if I appeared surly enough, I squeaked by in my role as just another bad guy. I had arranged for a fictitious address, some flophouse in Worcester and even managed to get a probationer's card showing me as having a conviction for armed robbery. That wasn't easy, believe me. The only weapon I carried was a 32-caliber Beretta automatic rolled up in my jeans in a handkerchief and my only I.D. was my badge pinned to the inside of my jeans. I figured if anyone ever got my pants off, it would be over for me anyway. Cautious or paranoid? You decide. Actually with my three or four day beard, sometimes Audrey would refuse to be seen in church with me.

During the time we were attempting to score drugs coming out of this bar in Fitchburg, I had a prosecution case in Firtchburg District Court. While waiting for my case to be called, properly dressed in a suit and tie, of course, I sat there while all the drunks were arraigned first. Who was part of the drunk tank? Right. My burglar from the bar. I was able to duck in time and he didn't see me. Like I said, "The good Lord watches over cops and drunks."

Within the next couple of weeks while working undercover in the bar, Wilbur my suspect pharmacist from up the street-showed up. We never really got close enough to him to observe him dealing in illegal drugs but I heard him telling someone he was going to a club in the nearby City of Leominster that Saturday night. So I arranged to be there with policewoman Grace O'Dell. May I add that Grace was one of the most astute female cops I have ever had the pleasure to work with. While dancing with Wilbur, Grace made a buy from him, a vial of amphetamines purchased illegally without a prescription. After she excused herself, she met me outside the club where I verified the drugs and placed them in an evidence envelope. I then went back to the club, tapped. Wilbur on the shoulder, identified myself and asked him to meet me outside for a. moment. We then arrested him for the sale of illegal drugs, a felony, and while transporting him to the Leominster Barracks, questioned him. He emphatically denied ever stealing or illegally selling dangerous drugs. Grace then picked up the evidence envelope containing the drugs he had sold her, using only her thumb and forefinger, and asked Wilbur what would happen when we dusted the vial for fingerprints. Of course the chances of getting his fingerprints off the vial were almost nil but Wilbur replied, "Okay. I guess you got me.'" He made a full admission, was prosecuted, and lost both his job and his pharmacist's license as well.

As previously mentioned, from time to time I was pulled back into uniform when an emergency or urgent situation arose and in the fall of 1961, I ended up in the search for the Coyle brothers. The Coyle brothers, after committing a robbery, shot and killed a Philadelphia policeman. They then kidnapped a motorist, forced him into the trunk of his car and proceeded toward Cape Cod, Massachusetts, a distance of about 300 miles. In Carver, Massachusetts, near Cape Cod, a Massachusetts State Trooper spotted the license plates given out on the all-points bulletin and pursued the vehicle, attempting to apprehend the two cop killers. In fact, not realizing that the rightful owner of the vehicle was in the trunk, the trooper fired two or three rounds into the trunk, of the car. Fortunately, the shots missed the poor soul inside. Realizing that they were in big trouble, the Coyle brothers abandoned their stolen car and fled into a very heavily wooded area which extended several square miles. A perimeter was then set up by troopers, local officers and FBI Agents and the search was on. It was decided to establish a search party headed by State Police Lieutenant Dick Tonis who was a well-decorated ex-Marine and a legend in his own time. A party of twelve officers, including two FBI Agents, was formed and not only was I included but got stuck with a Rising submachine gun. Man! That sucker was heavy. We proceeded into the woods at a jogging pace and ran for several miles but without success.

I can recall at one point, only Lieutenant Tonis and I were left, all others having given up due to exhaustion. At one point Tonis and I hit a clearing. Of course it was pitch dark and good old "Lonesome George" stepped into a gopher hole. The machinegun went one way and I went face down the other way. I then heard a half a dozen rifle bolts click, looked up and saw my coworkers around the perimeter aiming at me, not realizing who I was. I yelled, "State Police" just in time I think.

After having no results by about 3:00 AM, Lieutenant Tonis and I, all that was left of the search party, were relieved by other troopers and I made my way back home very proud of myself for having been one of two to have survived that run. I was tired but otherwise felt great. I was 32 years old at the time. But my vanity vanished after four or five hours sleep. My legs were so sore it took me a half hour to get out of bed. So much for macho-ism, huh?

The Coyle brothers' demise came at daybreak that same morning when another search party located them hiding in the woods. One brother opened fire on a trooper and the trooper returned fire, killing him. The other brother immediately surrendered, and was returned to Philadelphia and prosecuted for murder and kidnapping. I subsequently learned that my search party was within ten feet of where the Coyle brothers had been hiding. Lonesome George had dodged another bullet, literally.

One of the saddest experiences I had while assigned to the state police Narcotics Unit occurred in the town of Gardner. While checking drugstore records there for suspicious prescriptions, I noted that one pharmacy had an unusual number of prescriptions for Demerol, a synthetic narcotic, all written by one doctor, an M.D. He was employed and resided at the Gardner State Hospital. The pharmacist offered that perhaps the doctor was treating a terminal cancer patient. This could have been true but of course I was obligated to check it out. Unfortunately, this was not the case and when interviewed, the doctor readily admitted being addicted to Demerol and I had to arrest him. He was placed in the Gardner Police Department's jail pending arraignment the next morning. This doctor was a former captain in the famous 82nd Airborne Division, was well decorated and had a wife and small children. But unfortunately that arraignment at Gardner District Court never occurred because at about 2:00 AM the next morning, the duty officer at the Gardner Police Department called me at my home expressing concern that the doctor was having severe withdrawal problems, banging his head against the bar doors of his cell. He requested that the doctor, for his own safety, be admitted to the Worcester State Hospital for treatment. I readily agreed. Forty-eight hours later, the doctor was dead. Actually, in dealing with this case, I had no choice other than the action I took, but for years it really bothered me. A cop's life is not always easy or pleasant, believe me! Maybe I should point out here that this occurred long before any real help was available for addicts. At that time the federal government did have a facility available at Lexington, Kentucky, but feedback from addicts who were treated there was not very positive.

TWELVE

I now had a little over seven years with Massachusetts State Police. On one of my cases I had occasion to work with Special Agent Joe Boyle of the Treasury Department's Alcohol, Tobacco and Firearms Division, then part of IRS. As always, a certain amount of "cop talk" took place, comparing salaries, benefits and working conditions. As we compared notes so to speak, I realized the benefits enjoyed by federal law enforcement officers were extremely attractive. Massachusetts State Troopers had no tenure and although not really a problem, troopers had to reenlist every two years. But at the time, the promotional system was a mess. Theoretically, promotions were given by seniority but in reality were achieved through political contacts of which I had none. At that time, I had been recommended for promotion twice but to no avail. The threat, be it only veiled, of ending up back as a "barracks rat" on uniformed patrol and living in the barracks worried me. It worried Audrey too. So eventually I decided to apply for the position of U.S. Treasury Agent.

The Treasury Department allowed experience to substitute for a college degree and although I had not yet earned my Bachelor's degree, I was okay there. It also required passing a four-hour examination which was really a tough one. It included a math test, primarily dealing with problems to be solved by high school algebra equations, an English test including extensive vocabulary questions and two Observation and Perception tests. In one test, the applicant was given an eight by ten inch photograph of a normal street scene. After the applicant had viewed the scene for about five minutes, the photograph was taken away with no notes permitted. The applicant was then asked such questions as what was the license plate number on the vehicle in the far left corner of the photo or furnish the description of the pedestrian in the lower right hand corner of the photo.

In the second Observation and Perception test, the applicant was given an eight by ten inch photo of an office interior. Again, after five minutes the photo was taken away with no notes allowed. Then the applicant was given a 45-minute math test followed by questions from the Observation and Perception test on the office interior photo. Questions included how many desks and typewriters appeared in the photo, how many telephones in the office and describe the physical appearance and dress of the female clerk at the bottom of the photo.

As it worked out, on the date I was scheduled to take the examination at the Worcester Federal Building at 8:30 AM, I had been previously detailed to work the 10:00 PM to 8:00 AM shift at our headquarters radio room, replacing a civilian employee who had called in sick. With no sleep that night, I took the test and of course flunked miserably. No excuses, Lonesome George. But since I never could accept failure, I was crushed. I was not allowed to take the text again for another year so during that time I studied and I mean I really studied. By the time I took the test again I had my high school algebra down solid and had vocabulary coming out my ears. This time I passed.

Now, another major decision. I had eight years with Massachusetts State Police. I loved the outfit, especially my assignment with our Narcotics Unit. I liked the people I worked with and enjoyed both prosecuting cases and being qualified as an expert witness, much to the chagrin of defense attorneys. At the time, all appointments for U.S. Treasury Agent were made through the U.S. Civil Service Commission and included ATF, U.S. Customs, Secret Service, the IRS Criminal Investigation Division for tax fraud investigations and the fairly new Internal Affairs Division. The latter conducted investigations mostly dealing with allegations of public corruption or integrity problems.

When an agency had a vacancy for U.S. Treasury Agent, a joint oral board was held to interview all qualified or interested applicants. I was called to appear before ATF, Federal Bureau of Narcotics and Internal Affairs who had vacancies. ATF did not especially interest me as this was before the Federal Gun Control Act of 1968 and its jurisdiction was limited to enforcing the laws dealing with stolen cigarettes and liquor stills which were usually found in our southern states. (These were mostly wiped out by discount liquor stores.) Among the oral board officials interviewing me was the Regional Director of Federal Bureau of Narcotics, Mike Pacini. I knew Mike well as his agents and I worked a number of cases together. Mike was an honest and sincere person and I had great respect for him.

After my interview, Mike called me out into the hall adjacent to the interview room and offered me a job. Knowing that agency's reputation for transferring Special Agents quite frequently, I asked Mike what the chances of my remaining in the Boston field office were. And Mike, being the honest and direct kind of guy I knew him to be, replied, "Six months and then to New York City or Los Angeles." I knew this would never go over at home as neither Audrey nor my dad, who I had great respect for, were encouraging me toward a career change, especially at a reduction in salary and possible relocation. So I reluctantly turned Mike's offer down and as I was to find out later it was a wise decision. My only choice left at the time was to go with Internal Affairs. I was not exactly excited about investigating IRS employees who took too many coffee breaks or showed up late for work occasionally. I was assured that these were administrative matters and Internal Affairs concerned itself with only criminal matters. At the time, I had been recommended for a state police promotion again. However, the promotion went to a trooper with only two years on the job but whose brother happened to be a State Representative. I guess that did it for me. I accepted the offer of U.S. Treasury's Internal Affairs Division in Boston. A happy memory followed. I had accumulated 36 days off with the Massachusetts State Police and Audrey and I packed up our two kids and enjoyed a long awaited vacation in southern Florida for a month. It was the best vacation we ever had and the memory of it lives with all of us today.

THIRTEEN

I was now a big shot U.S. Treasury Agent. Right? Actually I was bored stiff. I worked only a 40 hour week and night after night found myself pacing up and down our driveway. As a state trooper, I never had any free time, never had time for hobbies, spending all available time with my wife and our two young ones. No more prosecution cases and no more chasing scumbags peddling dope. The only ego trip I had enjoyed was that when I was selected for Internal Affairs, they had two vacancies but were then cut back to one. (Typical government, I was to learn.) It had been a choice between a recent graduate Magna Cum Laude from Boston College or me and because of my criminal experience, I was selected. The Magna Cum Laude was picked up by ATF where he served about three years before marrying. His new wife then put him through law school and the last I'd heard he was making a small fortune on Wall Street in Admiralty Law.

At the time, the Treasury Department's Internal Affairs Division was relatively a newcomer to the Federal law enforcement community. The agency had been created by President Harry Truman with an attempt to bring more integrity to government. Although it had been in existence for about ten years, the agency had only been certified as a Federal Law Enforcement Agency with powers of arrest under Title 18 of the U.S. Criminal Code for about two years. Consequently when it had been initially staffed, there were very few people with any prior law enforcement experience. The Boston office which had about 20 agents, had only three former FBI Agents who wanted out of their New York field office and one former Connecticut State Trooper So we were really hurting for experience.

While learning the ropes and becoming familiar with all the government regulations and bureaucracy, quite an experience believe me, my first year in Internal Affairs left me wondering if I had made a mistake changing agencies. I missed the street action. But I was soon saved by the downfall of three New York City Federal Bureau of Narcotics Agents who had run amok.

It seemed that our New York City office had received information from a confidential informant whom I suspect had been caught "dirty," that a Federal Bureau of Narcotics agent was selling confiscated marijuana and heroin on the street. The information was forwarded to the Secretary of Treasury who immediately directed a full investigation be conducted to resolve the allegation. We subsequently found that not one but three Federal Bureau of Narcotics Agents and two nearby Nassau County officers were selling drugs on the street.

Now as everyone knows, all drugs to be used as evidence in a criminal proceeding must first be analyzed to determine whether the drugs are in fact illegal drugs as alleged. Normally, the drugs would be sent to the FBI's laboratory in Washington, D.C. for analysis This investigation of course involved federal agents selling narcotics on the street, a very sensitive case. In order to prevent a turf battle, and unfortunately they do exist to some extent, it was decided that maybe our agency should have the drugs analyzed elsewhere and an alternative was sought. A civilian analyst would not be appropriate. Enter Lonesome George.

Our chief, well aware of my background with Massachusetts State Police, quietly approached me one day and asked whether I had any discrete contacts with my former employer and if so, might the state police laboratory in Boston consider analyzing any drugs purchased from agents by our informant. The chief was very mindful that a Federal out-of-state law enforcement agency submitting drugs to Massachusetts State Police laboratory for analysis might raise a few eyebrows. The last thing we needed was a leak which, of course, would severely hamper our case.

This was probably a break for my career. While with the state police's Narcotic Unit I had been a steady customer at their lab. In fact the primary chemist and I had become good friends over the years. So I approached the Colonel of Massachusetts State Police who knew of my career change and who knew me personally when he had been a sergeant assigned to Troop C. I advised the Colonel that I was working on a very sensitive case ordered by the Secretary of Treasury and that the case involved illegal drugs which needed to be analyzed. I asked him whether we could use a state police analyst without a lot of exposure. The Colonel immediately responded that he did not want to know any of the facts involved and that I should feel free to solicit the services of the state police chemist with whom I had previously worked with. The chemist not only readily agreed to analyze all drugs submitted by me but really stuck his neck out, advising me the drugs submitted for analysis would not even be logged in, lest someone would notice and raise questions. My Chief was delighted with this arrangement.

During the following three or four months, when drugs had been purchased by informants from federal agents and county officers in New York, they were flown in by one of our New York based agents to Boston's Logan Airport and handed over to me. I transported them directly to the state police analyst in Boston. All drugs submitted were found to contain heroin or marijuana. As we suspected, when the case broke it received a lot of notoriety because the defendants were all law enforcement officers. The state police analyst ended up testifying in Southern District Court of New York and all federal and county officers were convicted. I ended up babysitting the informants at a military installation on Governors Island in New York for a week while they testified, as word was out there was a contract out on them. With the Statue of Liberty on the horizon, the scenery was beautiful, but I was guarding lowlifes and couldn't wait to get off that detail.

Reflecting back, when the Federal Bureau of Narcotics in Boston had offered me a job and I declined, the good Lord had been with me. Had I elected to accept the position, I would have been transferred to New York City, would probably have been exposed to all that corruption and after relocating would have ended up looking for another job. In fact a close friend of mine, John Krepheim, had fallen into that trap. He was hired by Federal Bureau of Narcotics in New York and the first week while working in Harlem, his partner had directed him to stop their vehicle outside a tenement. He told John to wait in the car and ten minutes later returned with a handful of cash. He held out some of it to John saying, "That's half." John replied, "What's this?" and the agent said, "Don't ask questions. That's your half." John refused and was subsequently treated by other agents in his squad as a leper. He thought about reporting the incident to his supervisor but was reluctant to do so. He decided to transfer to our Internal Affairs Division. That was a wise move because his DEA supervisor was eventually indicted on public corruption charges. Good move John.

While stationed in Boston, another interesting case evolved which I became apart of. It seemed that a middle-aged, single and very religious lady was the secretary of a former high level official in the Criminal Investigation Division of IRS (then known as the Intelligence Division). Her boss retired under pressure and was now representing local organized crime people.

At that time, under federal law, all bookmakers could conduct their bookmaking operations legally if they registered as such with IRS, even though bookmaking was a violation of state law. Of course most bookmakers were reluctant to register for fear of being targeted by local law enforcement. Consequently IRS's CID made periodic raids on unregistered bookmaker establishments. However it seemed that when a raid was conducted by agents, when they arrived at the scene, nobody was there. Obviously the bookmakers had been tipped off.

We had received information from a reliable source that the leak was in the office of the current Chief, CID. You guessed it. The leak was the chief's secretary who was still in love with her former boss and would tip him off whenever a raid was being planned. It seemed he would tip off organized crime people and that was an embarrassment to CID agents.

With the cooperation of CID's current chief who was a very concerned and unhappy man, we placed a legal wiretap on his secretary's office phone and a second one on a public telephone just outside her office. Both phones were monitored by Internal Affairs and if you think this was fun work, believe me it's not. The secretary was smart enough to use the public phone but most conversations we monitored were husbands telling their wives they were running late or single guys trying to line up a date. Naturally these conversations were not recorded and when I got stuck with this detail, I would return to my endless paperwork.

The secretary was put under an 18-hour surveillance by another Special Agent and me. Overtime in those days was nonexistent but the case was interesting. It went on for about two months and was unproductive until we surveilled her in the North End of Boston meeting her old boss for dinner. We were unable to overhear any conversation but did observe her handing over a document to him. Interesting. Subsequently a plan was developed to culminate the case.

Again, with the cooperation of the Chief, CID, a fake raid on bookmakers was created by a memorandum signed by the Chief, CID. Late one night, posing as telephone repair people, another Special Agent and I entered the federal building that housed CID and replaced the mirror in the copy room with a two-way mirror.

The following morning, the Chief, CID gave the memo to his secretary with specific instructions to make one copy only and return the original and one copy to him. Through the two-way mirror, we observed her making two copies of the memo. She gave her chief the original and one copy. We then kept her under continuous surveillance. After work she was observed meeting her lover, her old boss in CID. That was enough for us. The case was wrapped up pretty quickly and referred to the U.S. Attorney for prosecution. End of leak.

FOURTEEN

Under the supervision of our Boston Office of Internal Affairs, there was a two-agent office in Hartford, Connecticut. One of the Special Agents in Hartford had decided to venture into private industry and a vacancy existed there. At this point in time, my dad had retired as a Lieutenant with the Newton Fire Department and my folks had relocated to central Florida. Audrey's folks had retired to Cape Cod, Massachusetts and by that time we had adopted a third baby, a girl. Both of our families were now pretty much separated and we decided that applying for a Resident Agent's job in Hartford might be a good career move. I applied and the transfer was approved. So we relocated to Wethersfield near Hartford and settled down to a life in Connecticut, a beautiful and well-run state.

While stationed in Hartford, I received information that two ATF Agents had been attempting to develop a confidential informant late one night in a Hartford bar. Allegedly, as they were meeting the confidential informant there, a fight broke out and one of the agents suffered severe dental injuries. He was treated at a local hospital and was claiming Federal reimbursement for dental bills. The agent's office was questioning the claim and the matter was referred to Internal Affairs.

Naturally, my first step was to interview the two agents separately, getting affidavits from both. They both gave statements that they were on duty at the time of the altercation and while interviewing their confidential informant, a fight broke out, injuring one agent. Both advised that the incident could be corroborated by the Hartford PD who had responded to the incident.

After reading the Hartford PD incident report which didn't tell me much except that one agent received injuries, I attempted to interview the officer who had responded. Although very polite, he refused to give me a statement without permission of his chief. I had encountered the "thin blue line" once again. Not surprising of course. I then interviewed the Chief of the Hartford Police Department and after some flag waving he said he would allow the officer to give me a statement.

In his statement, the Hartford officer said that both agents claimed they were on official business at the bar, that both were slightly inebriated but no action had been taken and the matter was considered by the Hartford PD to be closed.

Since both agents had identified their confidential informant by name, I began to search for him. That wasn't easy! I finally determined that by occupation, he was a roofer. Swell! After more searching, one day I tracked him down up on a roof in East Hartford. I called him down to where I could talk to him privately and he told me he had known both agents personally for a long time. I specifically asked him whether he ever provided either agent with information on criminal activity. He replied that he had not and in fact didn't know of any such information. He said that he knew both agents socially through a bar they frequented. He gave me an affidavit to this effect. Both agents were then interviewed back to back, so to speak, and both stuck to their original statements. Both were removed from office. They appealed to the U.S. Civil Service Commission who upheld the Treasury Department's decision to remove them. One of the agent's father had been a high level ATF official at the time, which must have been most embarrassing for his dad.

Another interesting case was assigned to me wherein a taxpayer we shall refer to as Brett had a problem with IRS. He owed money on his taxes. Those not familiar with IRS practices should know that if a taxpayer owes money, after a number of phone calls and written correspondence, the collection of tax is referred by a TDA (Taxpayer Delinquent Account) to a Revenue Officer for collection. The Revenue Officer then contacts the taxpayer to arrange for the collection of the delinquent tax, if possible. According to the Revenue Officer's documentation, he had contacted the taxpayer who said he would try to raise the money to pay IRS, but thus far, no money had been paid.

The taxpayer, Brett, had authored a letter to IRS claiming that on a certain date, he met with the assigned Revenue Officer, gave him $500 in cash toward his delinquent account but was given no receipt. In fact he specifically stated in the letter that he gave the Revenue Officer "five crisp new $100 bills." But the account history attached to the taxpayer's TDA, stated that no money had been received on that date.

I finally located the taxpayer, Brett, in the Danvers, Connecticut area and interviewed him. He told me that he had given the Revenue Officer $500 but had received no receipt and the money was never credited to his account. I then asked him, specifically, if he remembered the currency denominations he had given the Revenue Officer and he replied that the money had been in $20s and $10s as he had to scurry around to scrape it up. He gave me a sworn affidavit to this effect. I thought to myself, "Brett, you just made a huge mistake. Not only have you tried to cheat Uncle Sam out of $500 but in doing so, have implied that an honest government employee had violated his integrity, stealing money."

Based on the confliction between Brett's letter to the IRS and his sworn statement to me as to the denomination of the currency involved, I referred the case to the United States Attorney in Hartford who agreed to prosecute Brett under Title 18, Section 1,001, Making a False Statement to a Government Official, which is a felony. Ironically, before the trial commenced, the Revenue Officer involved resigned from the IRS to join the clergy. I tried to persuade the Assistant U.S. Attorney prosecuting the case to allow the former Revenue Officer to wear his newly acquired clergymen's habit but he just laughed and said he thought it might be overkill. Unfortunately, the defendant waived a jury trial and the judge, who had a reputation for being anti-IRS found the defendant not guilty. When subsequently questioned by the Assistant U.S. Attorney, he replied, "It was only $500." After all that effort, I was pissed but at least we had preserved the integrity of an honest government employee which was satisfying.

I also participated in the saga of a former French Underground guy from World War II. Now a U.S. citizen, a gentleman from Norwalk, Connecticut, near the New York state line, wrote a letter to IRS complaining that his New York based accountant had advised him he was now under audit by the IRS and the accountant had told him he would settle a substantial adjustment from the audit of his tax return if the taxpayer would come up with $1,500 to pay off the Revenue Agent assigned to his audit. The taxpayer, now a successful businessman, was naturally very upset.

The case was referred to Internal Affairs and when we interviewed the taxpayer, he reiterated what he had written to IRS. He said he had relocated to the United States from his native France where he had been active in the French Underground. This, of course, if true, had nothing to do with being shaken down by an allegedly corrupt Revenue Agent but I have yet to meet any older Frenchman who did not tell me he was involved in the underground movement during World War II.

At any rate, after listening to the taxpayer's story about his accountant being able to pay off an Internal Revenue Service employee $1,500 to dodge a $10,000 tax liability, we felt we had sufficient probable cause to go for a wire and were so authorized by Washington, D.C. We arranged for the taxpayer's accountant to meet him at his palatial residence in Norwalk on a certain date and wired up the living room to record any conversation at that meeting where the accountant would advise his client of the IRS payoff. Interestingly enough, IRS records showed that in fact the taxpayer was not under audit at all. It appeared the accountant was just trying to shake down his wealthy client for a fast buck.

The accountant showed up for the interview which we monitored from an upstairs bedroom. But the accountant became evasive and never actually stated he had a Revenue Agent on the take. The taxpayer never paid the accountant the $1,500, changed to another accountant and we closed our case. With no real proof, we were unable to refer the matter to the State Board of Accountancy and no further action was taken.

I can remember a very sad case I investigated while assigned to the Hartford . office. It occurred in Pittsfield, Massachusetts, where a family of modest income were selected for audit by IRS. I don't recall exactly what the tax issue was but these people were certainly not affluent by any means. As it happened, when the husband and wife appeared at the IRS office for their audit, they had their 12-year-old son with them. That is the boy was 12 years old physically but he was mentally challenged. The IRS auditor was a 30-year-old white male. During the interview, the auditor appeared to be very friendly to the youngster. He told the boy's parents he had always wanted a younger brother but it never happened.

After the audit concluded, the auditor started visiting the couple's mentally challenged son at home and they assumed he was interested in developing a "big brother" type relationship. With their permission the auditor started to take the boy to different places around Pittsfield. Since he appeared to be a responsible government employee in a position of trust with the IRS they were not concerned. But when the boy started coming home with stories that the auditor had been touching him and fondling him, they became concerned and reluctantly made a complaint to IRS. The complaint was promptly referred to Internal Affairs and I got the case.

Experience had taught me that not everyone was exactly in love with IRS and this could be just another frivolous complaint. So I immediately interviewed both the parents and the boy separately. Although the youngster was very difficult to interview because of his disability, there was no doubt in my mind that it was no frivolous complaint. In fact it was worse than I had assumed. After interviewing the parents, I found the auditor had not just fondled the boy but had sexually molested him.

I then interviewed the auditor who immediately admitted molesting the boy and after our interview, he went directly to IRS's Personnel office and resigned. I subsequently advised the boy's parents that they could pursue state criminal charges but they declined.

FIFTEEN

Although Connecticut is a nice state in which to raise a family, as an Internal Affairs Agent, I was bored. Not enough action for me anyway. I missed grass roots law enforcement. I still had not learned to stop and smell the roses. At that time, the Federal Bureau of Narcotics under U.S. Treasury was being phased out and what is now DEA (Drug Enforcement Agency) was being formed under our U.S. Justice Department. I decided to take a shot at it and my wife as understanding as ever, agreed. So I took a couple of days leave and Audrey and I loaded the kids into the car and headed for Washington, D.C. While they took in the sights there, I had an appointment with DEA's new Director. With my background and experience I felt confident they would offer me a job. I was wrong. I had been mistaken in that what seemed like a very receptive Director turned out to be just another bureaucratic smile. I learned much later that a deal between DEA and Treasury's Internal Affairs had quietly been cut that Internal Affairs would not be raided of its Special Agents.

About six months later, I was offered a promotion back at our Boston office and Audrey and the kids were anxious to get closer to Grandma and Grandpa, so we relocated to Needham, Massachusetts, just outside of Boston. We found a beautiful home there at a great price. We had just settled in when I was detailed to Newark, New Jersey where a very sensitive case was surfacing.

Information had been received that three very high level IRS officials in Newark were having an unhealthy relationship with certain organized crime figures. At that time Gerado Cantena, counterpart to New York's Joe Columbo, was alleged to be the "Don" in New Jersey with a lieutenant by the name of Phil Dameo. All three IRS officials were alleged to be receiving financial benefits from certain organized crime people with the assumption that they would be free of any problems with IRS. In fact the wife of one official was on the payroll of a trucking company with organized crime connections as a comparison shopper, if you will. She had no office and was never seen working there. Just a coincidence I guess.

Now the investigation was expanding and would include a 15-hour surveillance of these three suspected officials in an attempt to connect them with what is described in the IRS Code of Conduct as "disreputable persons."

An elaborate undercover operation was set up and using a fictitious identity, Internal Affairs had ten agents rent vehicles from a small rental agency in New Jersey. We were given false identity cards and told not to carry our Treasury I.D. cards or our weapons, that if we were arrested for some reason by another law enforcement agency, our headquarters would respond that they never heard of us. Comforting, huh? Of course, personal survivorship comes first and I was never very far away from my weapon or my Treasury I. D card.

A 15-hour a day surveillance, seven days a week is always demanding. We had very little time off. In fact I was only allowed one day off every two weeks and faced a 200-mile trip home, each way. But by now Internal Affairs had what was called unscheduled overtime. Technically you could be required to work 24 hours a day for the same money but that didn't happen very often. Money-wise it did help. Food, again like in all surveillances, was also a problem. It was catch as catch can and then mostly junk food. In order to avoid suspicion we had to change lodging every three days or so as Newark in those days did not enjoy a very good reputation as far as public corruption went.

I can recall on one occasion, we had changed lodging accommodations in the Newark area, found a rather decent hotel at a good rate, checked in and a meeting was called. As we all gathered in the room of one Special Agent, I entered to find several weapons laying on his bed including a rifle, a shotgun and an Uzi semi-automatic. Apparently this Special Agent was just a gun nut. Why would he have such weaponry in his possession on such an operation was beyond me. As we started our meeting, the hotel cleaning lady entered unannounced, took one look at the weaponry on the bed and fled. Of course we immediately checked out and were forced to find lodging elsewhere. Incidentally, the agent with all those weapons subsequently transferred to an agency where he would be more comfortable. Certainly we were more comfortable.

The surveillance lasted from January through March and the northeast part of our country had some pretty severe weather that year, which

made surveillance difficult. In fact, once we were hit with snowstorms total-
ing over three feet. I happened to be off duty at home at the time.
Anticipating a travel problem back to the Newark area, a distance of about
200 miles, I left home at about 3:00 AM and did not arrive at my lodging
until eight hours later. Normally it would take only four hours. Literally, one
could not see the roofs of other vehicles approaching an intersection.

It became a problem at home too. I was away from home for over
two months leaving Audrey alone to cope with three small children.
Although uncomplaining at the time, she has since reminded me of that
winter many times. The life of a cop's wife is not always an easy one.

We surveilled our suspects from the time they left their homes in
the morning until lights went out at night. Every night. If they met other
people, we surveilled them too until they could be identified and eliminated
as being pertinent to our investigation. Overall, the surveillance produced
very few leads for other agents to follow up on. Given the resources that
were being expended and the cost involved, the surveillance was called off
in early March and Audrey and I were relieved to return to a normal life.
That is normal for any law enforcement officer. But it was short lived.
Information had been received that one IRS official's daughter was about to
be married and a wedding reception was to be held in Short Hills, New
Jersey. Feeling this might be the last shot we had in connecting the official
to organized crime, it was decided to reactivate the surveillance. Another
agent and I were assigned to cover the wedding reception.

We were told that at the risk of being identified or suspected, we
were to take that chance if our observations were productive. We stationed
our rental car a short distance away from The Arch Restaurant in Short Hills
where the wedding reception was being held until about 11:30 PM. As we
were sitting in our vehicle, a Short Hills police officer pulled up. Naturally
seeing two guys in suits and ties, he asked what we were doing at this hour
parked in a nearby parking lot. We produced our phony credentials.
Although he didn't really know who we were, he smelled "cop," gave us a
big grin and said, "See ya." Shortly thereafter, I made the decision to go into
the restaurant and observe the wedding party which was still very much
ongoing. We entered, became seated and who do we see seated with our suspect IRS official but Phil Dameo, Jerry Cantena's lieutenant. In fact, at one
point Phil even danced with the bride. I immediately telephoned the case
manager, John McManus and we had made our case. Surveillance was ter-
minated and I finally returned back home for good.

Well not exactly. About that time, a grade GS-13 position became
open in New York City. This grade, at least in Internal Affairs, is a key grade
leading to management if one desires that goal and after my wife and I dis-

cussed it at length, I decided to put in for it. This was apparently unique as no respectable Bostonian would ever venture out of "Bean Town," especially relocating to New York City. While I was being considered for the position, DEA called me and offered me a job in Boston. I politely (and very smugly I'm afraid) declined their offer, stating I was being considered for a promotion to New York. They told me that no Bostonian would ever be selected for a position in New York, that I would be very disappointed. I replied that I would take my chances. I did and I got the job.

SIXTEEN

After a meager six-day house-hunting trip, which at the time was all transferred government employees were allotted, we found an English Tudor home in Ridgewood, New Jersey. It had only one bathroom but the kids were small and otherwise it was really in good shape. Ridgewood is a delightful town located a short distance away from the George Washington Bridge connecting New York City to New Jersey. We found New York to be an interesting city and very unique. If one's luck is down, life can be miserable. But if one has a well paying and interesting job with further opportunity, it can be a great city. While Ridgewood is almost in a country setting and the kids enjoyed many a field trip to New York, I was in heaven. Although I had better than a ten hour work day, the cases were interesting and exciting. At that time, New York was leading the country in crime and in Internal Affairs, there was no exception, especially when dealing with IRS.

Don't get me wrong. The problem was not corruption in the IRS, although I found there was some, but generally quite the opposite. There were many attempted bribery cases where taxpayers or their accountants would attempt to bribe an IRS employee. In fact there was one occasion where I accompanied a new Internal Affairs Agent on his first arrest. It involved an accountant whose office was in lower Manhattan. After we told his secretary we wished to see him, she pointed to his office door and we entered. We identified ourselves and I said, "Mr. Goldberg? We have a warrant for your arrest for Bribery of a Public Official." Mr. Goldberg replied, "Which one?" Apparently IRS was not the only agency whose employees Mr. Goldberg had been bribing.

This was not an isolated case but just one of many. There were more attempted bribe cases reported by IRS in New York City than any other city in the country, at least at that time. Nationwide, Internal Affairs, in conjunction with IRS, had an ongoing Integrity Awareness program for all IRS field employees which included how to identify an offer of bribery (not all offers of bribery are that direct), how to respond and why they should immediately report the overture to Internal Affairs.

By way of explanation, Revenue Agents are not federal law enforcement officers but accountants by profession who conduct audits of federal income tax returns. In doing so, they have great latitude in determining what constitutes taxable income and what business expenses are allowable. They literally have nobody looking over their shoulders. They can be very vulnerable to potential bribe offers by taxpayers or their representatives, who, if you will, wish to beat the system. Experience had taught us that if an IRS employee merely turned down a bribe offer flatly, the taxpayer or accountant would again approach another employee with a similar offer. That employee might, for some unforgivable reason, accept the offer. By the very nature of their work, the Internal Revenue Service generally suffers a negative image by the American public. (Nobody likes to see an IRS employee at their door.) IRS deals with millions of dollars every year and considers attempted bribery almost an occupational hazard. The last thing it needs is a scandal involving IRS corruption. The news media would probably like it but not the Federal Government. So all IRS employees are still required to attend training on Integrity Awareness at least once annually. It must work because to my knowledge, there has never been a nationwide scandal involving corruption in the Internal Revenue Service.

In New York, we had a lot of attempted bribery of IRS employee cases in our inventory and most were fun to work. The only hazard in working a bribery case was eliminating the defense of entrapment. If the defendant could prove the government in some way encouraged the defendant to commit the crime, the defendant would in all probability, be found not guilty. On the other hand, if the government could prove it in no way encouraged the defendant to commit the crime, there was no defense of entrapment available and a conviction would be probable. Usually we were able to eliminate the defense of entrapment by recording all conversations of the parties involved with the permission of one party, that party being the cooperating IRS employee who reported the attempted bribe. Internal Affairs had a 90% conviction rate on bribery cases which we were certainly proud of.

One never knew what to expect when working a bribe case, especially in New York City. In fact at this stage of my life, I am a firm believer in "Murphy's Law." I can recall one case where we wired up the Revenue Agent as usual and sent him in to the suspect accountant's office located just outside of Manhattan's Times Square. It was not the best neighborhood in town. The Revenue Agent had been briefed as always, not to bring up the previously made bribe offer but let the accountant do so, thereby eliminating any defense of entrapment. Of course, he was also told to stick to the tax issue and not get off on the New York Yankees or how the Giants were doing, that all conversations must be transcribed prior to trial which was a very laborious task. Usually when a defendant's attorney heard our taped conversations between his client and our cooperating employee, he would throw up his hands and his client would plead guilty, but only on the date of the scheduled trial. In event a trial did occur, we still had to be prepared.

As we were sitting in our car, monitoring and recording the Revenue Agent's conversation with the accountant, just below the accountant's office we witnessed an assault with intent to Commit Murder happening about 50 yards away on a street corner. Some guy was standing there waiting for a pedestrian light when another guy approached him, pulled out a six inch knife and gutted him. This was at about 11:00 in the morning on a business day. Obviously a drug deal gone bad. Anyway, the victim went down and there was blood everywhere. Under other circumstances we would have jumped out of our car, apprehended the assailant and aided the victim. But we were conducting a federal felony investigation and were responsible for the Revenue Agent's safety, I could envision the accountant peering out of his office window trying to see what all the commotion on the street below was all about and spotting us. As it turned out, NYPD showed up almost immediately and took care of the situation. In those days uniformed officers patrolled the streets of Time Square, three abreast. It helped some. Anyway, the accountant's bribe offer was repeated and we made our case.

My promotion to New York City as a grade GS-13 was not in a supervisory capacity but as a Special Assistant to our Chief. This meant I was still on the street as an agent but with more complicated cases. Although I thoroughly enjoyed all the action, my goal was to eventually end up in management. However, not quite yet. In fact it seemed my specialty if any, was surveillance as around that time, I caught another one. Just like everyone else, IRS has attorneys too. They call them Regional Counsel and are located in every headquarters of IRS. In New York City there were a number of them. One such attorney whom we will refer to as Bert Kline had retired under a cloud, so to speak. Information had been received that Bert, while with IRS had been taking bribes to influence IRS cases. A financial investigation conducted by Internal Affairs thus far seemed to indicate there was merit to the allegation. A surveillance was needed to establish his current activity and Special Agent Bill Silverman and I were assigned. Kline lived in Nassau County on Long Island and worked out of an office building just off Times Square. The building was well known to Internal Affairs and we had dubbed it "the den of thieves." Need I say more about its reputation with us?

Bill turned out to be one of the best street agents I have ever had the pleasure of working with and we became close friends over the years. As with most surveillances the hours were long with the usual missing of meals. I had to get up at 3:00 in the morning, pick up an undercover car at our office in Foley Square in lower Manhattan, meet Bill and drive to Kline's residence on Long Island to await his departure there for who knew where. Usually he departed at about 6:30 AM for the "den of thieves" but we never knew. As one might think, a surveillance in New York City with all that traffic, could be demanding, regardless of what you see in the movies coming out of Hollywood. There were several occasions when we lost him, at least temporarily.

Initially we were using a seized late model Cadillac convertible which really worked out-well since Kline lived in a rather affluent neighborhood and we blended into the area without attracting any attention.

Then one day, the Cadillac was needed on another assignment and we ended up in an unmarked Ford sedan, a typical "cop car." We weren't there 45 minutes when not one, not two but five Nassau County marked cars surrounded us. A sergeant approached our car and seeing two guys in suits and ties in a plain black Ford sedan, knew we didn't appear to be burglars as some neighbor had reported. We identified ourselves and told him we were on an investigation. He smiled and returned to his car but another officer asked us what kind of case were we working. I replied, "A federal case." He gave me a rather disgusted look and left, probably muttering to himself "Dammed Feds."

On another occasion, Bill and I were at Kline's residence early in the morning. Kline came out, drove to the Long Island Railroad Station, parked and boarded a train for Brooklyn. We knew he would in all probability switch in Brooklyn to a subway for Manhattan. I boarded the train to follow him on foot while Bill drove our car to the Brooklyn railway stop. I'm still not sure how he got there so quickly but when he arrived at the Brooklyn subway stop he saw Kline and me heading for the train there.

As anyone who has ever had to park a car in New York City knows, it's generally a hellacious problem. Bill had to dump our Cadillac in the nearest parking lot to join me in our foot surveillance. We followed Kline to Manhattan and he met with several people who might have been pertinent to our case. Finally, Kline grabbed a train to his residence on Long Island and Bill and I returned to our Cadillac in the Brooklyn parking lot.

Apparently, in his haste, and rightfully so, Bill had parked our car blocking two or three other cars. The parking lot attendant was furious. He refused to move two cars blocking us from leaving. After 15 hours on the street. Bill and I were both tired and neither of us was ready for this confrontation. Bill practically stuck his badge down the guy's throat and threatened to arrest him for Obstruction of Justice. That made matters worse. I finally got Silverman calmed down in our car and pointed out that it really was late. Did we want to arrest this guy and lug him all the way downtown to West Street in Manhattan to the lockup we used when necessary? Bill, still fuming, reluctantly agreed maybe that wasn't such a good idea. So he sat in our car while I went back to the attendant, apologized and he, probably not wanting to push his luck, agreed to move the two vehicles blocking our car. I started up our car and was preparing depart when Bill said, "Wait a minute!" He then jumped out of our car, went over to the parking lot attendant and yelled, "Why don't you go f... yourself!" Satisfied, Bill got back in our car. I just shook my head and we left. Another day and 3:00 AM would come soon enough. Too soon.

On another occasion. Bill and I were standing on opposite corners watching the "den of thieves" waiting for Kline to come out. Some big burly guy approached Silverman and said to him, "Who are you?" Bill said, "Who the hell are you?" and a little verbal contest ensued. As it turned out the guy was an NYPD detective. The building that housed Kline's office also housed a bank and someone had seen us standing there and assumed we were staking out the bank for a robbery. The detective really should have identified himself initially.

Bill and I maintained surveillance on Kline for almost a month. We worked well together, always anticipating each other's moves. Then one day I routinely called the case agent reporting our activities and he told me that they were taking Silverman off the surveillance and he was sending me someone else to replace him. I protested and said this was not the time for me to be breaking in a green agent. The case agent said he had not been part of the decision making, that they were replacing Silverman with Special Agent Art Findlay. He pointed out that Findlay had retired as a detective with NYPD. I said, "Oh well. Send him down." The case agent, knowing my background, chirped, "Yeah. Blood is thicker than water. Right?"

Art Findlay and I worked extremely well together and have remained friends ever since. In fact, I found him to be rather an expert on the "wise guys" (organized crime figures in New York). The case went on for about another month, leads were developed and the financial investigation showed Kline had about a million dollars in bribe money squirreled away in the Bahamas, tax free. He was prosecuted for tax evasion.

At the time of Kline's trial, a rather humorous incident popped up. We had been assisted with our financial investigation by an IRS Internal Auditor. In searching Kline's office, he had found some incriminating evidence in the way of bank records. His report of investigation was entered into evidence and the Internal Auditor was testifying for the government. He testified that he found the evidence in Kline's credenza. On cross-examination, Kline's defense attorney thought he would seize the opportunity to discredit the Internal Auditor's credibility as a witness. He said "Sir. Did you prepare the report of investigation bearing your name which now is in evidence?" The Internal Auditor replied, "Yes Sir." The attorney then said, "Well, how come you just testified that you found these bank records in the defendant's credenza when in fact according to your written report, you found them in his desk?" The Internal Auditor replied, "Because I couldn't spell credenza." This brought quite a chuckle from both the judge and jury.

As a Special Assistant to the Chief, I became a small part of a mammoth case code named "Project W" after Special Agent Harold Wenig. Harold was a retired NYPD detective out of Brooklyn and I must say he was some piece of work. In appearance, he gave off the perfect image that most people would envision as a New York detective. He was a big man, about 6 foot 2 inches weighing about 215 pounds and none of it was fat. He had a booming voice which he used quite often. I am certain that the bookmakers and other lowlifes in Brooklyn were very happy when Harold retired from NYPD because he was straight as an arrow and talk around the office was he would lock up his best friend if he caught him dirty. Not only was Harold a good cop but he had other qualities. He had imagination and was innovative, probably to the point where he could try the patience of any supervisor. All this about Harold was how Project W came about.

It seems that one day Harold was approached by an acquaintance who had talked to someone under investigation by Internal Affairs. The acquaintance had told Harold that he knew someone who was interested in accessing certain information in our Internal Affairs files and would pay pretty good money to get it. Harold took this to be the beginning of a bribe offer and of course, rightfully so. Why anyone would be so foolish as to offer a bribe to an Internal Affairs Special Agent? Well folks, in New York City, its different, or at least it was at that time. In fact in the previous two and a half years we had arrested 39 current or former IRS employees for accepting bribes. This severely damaged the reputation of the Internal Revenue Service in the northeast part of the United States where most of the problems had occurred and why we were so involved in conducting Integrity Awareness sessions. But nonetheless it looked like now someone was attempting to bribe one of our Internal Affairs people. So Harold told the guy to set up a meeting. Of course he immediately reported the bribe offer to our Chief.

Subsequently, an electronically wired Harold Wenig met with the suspect who turned out to be an IRS Revenue Agent who was under investigation by Internal Affairs. He offered Harold $250 for any information we might have on him and Harold agreed. At a subsequent meeting Wenig handed over information which had been doctored of course so it would not severely damage our case, and the agent paid Harold $250.

Now normally, after bribing a public official, when we are sure we have proof on our tapes, the person is immediately arrested. But as I indicated earlier Wenig was a very innovative person and he asked the agent if he knew anyone else who might want access to our confidential files. The agent said he would ask around.

Now in case you think Wenig's statement might be considered entrapment, it was not. The statement was not an inducement to commit a crime the person would not otherwise commit because the person had already committed a felony by bribing a Special Agent and was assuming the Special Agent was also corrupt. So after checking with the United States Attorney, Southern District of New York, it was decided it would be interesting to see just how many other people there were out there who were interested in Internal Affairs files for a price.

As we suspected, word got around and for the next 18 months, 22 current IRS employees, four former employees and a well-known CPA met with Special Agent Wenig clandestinely, of course, and paid him up to $2,500 each for information we had in our Internal Affairs files on them. All meetings were recorded on audio tape and some on video tape as well.

When Harold initially met with the CPA involved, the CPA was extremely nervous and refused to meet in the usual out of the way place, that being Harold's personal vehicle. Harold suggested they meet at the East River docks at night and the CPA agreed that would be a lot safer. A time and a place was set. This seemed like an ideal opportunity to get a close up shot of the payoff and our people rented a boat and set up a camera with a zoom lens and took up a position near the meeting. After the bribe went down, we were extremely pleased that we had filmed it all until our people got back to the office to develop the film and found that someone, through a slight miscommunication had not loaded the camera with film. Everyone in the office thought that was a riot except the guys who were on the boat.

To establish greater impact, it was decided to make an attempt at least to arrest all 27 suspects simultaneously in one day. With all the suspects residing in the five boroughs of New York City, Long Island and New Jersey, that was an ambitious plan to be sure. Special Agents from the

Boston, Buffalo and Albany offices were called in to assist, making a total of 75 agents in all.

Now do you remember the CPA we took a photo of without the film in our camera? Well this guy posed us another problem. When our two Special Agents went to arrest him in his mid-town Manhattan office, they parked their unmarked car outside his office, illegally of course. Usually, if the car's radio microphone is placed over the rear vision mirror and a government plate is placed on the dashboard, the meter maid will see it as a police car and ignore it. But not this time. When our people came out with the CPA, their car had been towed away. All our other cars were tied up making other arrests so they had no choice but to waltz the CPA still handcuffed to the nearest IRT subway and transport him downtown to the U.S. Marshall's Office where he was booked in. When we kidded them about this, they simply shrugged their shoulders and grinned saying, "Well, that's New York." Ironically, two FBI Agents were making an arrest on one of their cases just up the street and returned to find their car had been towed too. They were not so charitable.

The arrest that Special Agent Teddy Medwig and I made was a little different as well. We ended up on the front page of the New York Times. Our person to be arrested was a former IRS Revenue Agent who had resigned after 13 years and now practiced as an accountant in mid-town Manhattan. Our prior surveillance established that he left his home in Baldwin, New York about 9:00 AM each morning and headed for his office via the Long Island Railroad.

Now I have learned over the years that when I attempt to execute *a* federal arrest warrant, if at all possible, it is better to stay away from the inside of a person's residence. To do otherwise, exposes the agents to a screeching wife, an upset mother or kids covered with peanut butter and jelly trying to wrap themselves around your leg to prevent you from taking their daddy off to jail. It is also prudent to avoid fighting off the family dog.

So on the day of the multiple arrests, Teddy and I parked our unmarked car outside the residence of the person to be arrested shortly before 9:00 AM. At about 9:00 AM he came out of his house heading for his car parked in the driveway out front. I called to the man by name and he turned around and came toward us. We identified ourselves, advised him he was being arrested for Bribery of a Public Official, handcuffed him and read him his rights. We then placed him in the back seat of our vehicle and drove off to Manhattan where he was booked in at the U.S. Marshall's Office.

Neat and simple? We thought so. But, apparently the man's wife was observing all this from inside their residence. So she called Nassau County Police Department and reported that two well dressed men had just kidnapped her husband outside their home and drove off. Obviously she had seen us handcuff her husband but neglected to include that in her report to police who immediately sent out a teletype alarm. The kidnapping was almost immediately solved but Teddy and I did make the New York Times as two "nattily dressed gents." I guess it pays to dress well, huh?

Then there was "Project S" to get involved with. It started out with a Revenue Agent reporting a bribe offer from someone believed to be one of the wise guys, organized crime guys, that is. As the bribe offer unfolded, covered by Internal Affairs, I found one of the biggest snake pits of attempted public corruption I had ever witnessed in my law enforcement career thus far. The Revenue Agent who reported the initial bribe offer was of Italian decent. The wise guy who made the bribe offer was also of Italian extraction and went to great effort to establish a strong rapport with our cooperating employee who was encouraged by us to take advantage of it and play the role. The Mafia guy who thought he had found a friendly IRS Agent quickly spread the word to other organized crime figures who were also under IRS scrutiny. Our Revenue Agent then introduced another Revenue Agent who the Mafia people thought was on the take as well. Our investigation then spread to a retired Special Agent of IRS's Criminal Investigation Division who was representing organized crime people. He and two other Special Agents became involved in our case and were put under continuous surveillance for months. Enter Lonesome George again. If anyone thinks surveillances are fun, believe me they're not. Although they can be exciting at times, most of it involves spending eight or ten hours in a car or standing on a street corner, praying that your subject will go somewhere, anywhere, just to break up the day or night.

We finally caught one of our Special Agents dirty, interviewed him and faced with a long-term prison sentence, or so he thought, sang and sang loudly. We had turned him and he provided us with a lot of information involving other organized crime figures and their connection with IRS.

Under Project S, we also received information that a current CID Special Agent was on the take, fixing tax evasion prosecution cases. If I may elaborate, Special Agents of IRS's CID include in their reports of investigation, a recommendation as to whether the taxpayer (or should I say non-taxpayer) be criminally prosecuted for tax evasion. The case is then forwarded to an Assistant U.S. Attorney for consideration. If both CID and The U.S. Attorney's Office concur, the case is accepted for prosecution.

One day my chief yelled over the intercom on my desk, "Vuilleumier? Get into my office." This demand was not uncommon at all and I dropped everything and hightailed it in there. He had the Special Agent coordinating Project S with him.

Our chief said, "You're going undercover in the U.S. Attorney's Office for a couple of hours." He must have seen the puzzled look on my face as I said, "Whatever you say Chief." He continued, "I want you to pose as a U.S. Immigration officer, sitting in the U.S. Attorney's Office looking at a bunch of files. A CID Special Agent will get there pretty soon and present a tax evasion case. Listen to the conversation and take as many notes as possible. Okay?" As usual, my reply was, "Gotcha Chief."

I then reported to the rather small office of Assistant U.S. Attorney Bill Gilbreth whom I knew and who was expecting me. He reiterated that a CID Special Agent would show up in a few minutes to discuss a CID prosecution case, that he would only introduce me as an Immigration Officer who needed to look at some files. He then seated me at a small table about six or seven feet away from his desk, shoved a bunch of files in front of me which made no sense to me at all and I settled down.

About 30 minutes later a CID Special Agent arrived. Gilbreth introduced me to the Special Agent as an Immigration Officer looking through some files and thereafter I was ignored. The Special Agent then discussed a CID tax evasion case with Gilbreth, saying that his office was not too anxious to prosecute as they thought it was rather a weak case. Gilbreth replied that if CID thought it was a weak case, he would decline prosecution and the Special Agent left shortly thereafter. Having overheard the conversation and taken as many notes as possible, I returned to our office and related to our chief what I had overheard. He seemed pleased. I later learned that the Special Agent had returned to his office and had advised his supervisor that the U.S. Attorney's Office thought CID's case was weak and declined prosecution. It was then quite obvious. The Special Agent had fixed a prosecution case for a Mafia individual, probably at a good price. My role as an Immigration Officer was only to witness the conversation I had overheard as an unbiased witness not familiar with the allegation facing the agent. But in the end, justice prevailed and the Special Agent was prosecuted. I don't recall what happened to the Mafia guy's tax evasion case. It was probably tainted by then but the civil penalties are horrendous. I'm sure he paid dearly.

We then received information that the Mafia people suspected our cooperating IRS employees were no longer to be trusted and in fact there was supposed to be a contract out on them. So we formed a 24 hour protection detail for the employees and their families until arrests could be made. I drew one of these details and after spending eight hours on another case, I joined another Special Agent to accompany one of the employees to his residence for overnight protection. There were no problems on our shift but I had worked 38 hours straight, the longest day of my career. I finally returned home to find my son waiting for me. It seemed he had finally saved up enough money from his paper route to buy his own television set and was waiting for me to help him shop for it. Audrey protested but I weakened and off we went looking for a TV.

Eventually we arrested eight Mafia figures and two former IRS Special Agents in Project S. The Mafiosi included Nick Rattini and John Mascillo of the Vito Genovese family. Rattini had paid one of our cooperating Revenue Agents $4,500. Both Revenue Agents were promoted and at their request, transferred to Washington, D.C. Both were afraid of repercussions from organized crime people but none ever came.

SEVENTEEN

While stationed in New York, I had another interesting challenge come up. An allegation that the Chief of IRS's Criminal Investigation Division in Boston was receiving gratuities from local politicians. Anyone familiar with Boston politics can well understand the impact that might have on the Treasury Department's integrity if in fact there was any merit to the allegation. Normally, the matter would have been investigated by our Internal Affairs office in Boston, but probably the relationship between CID and Internal Affairs would be adversely affected for some time thereafter. Therefore it was decided that Internal Affairs in New York would attempt to resolve the allegation. Three Special Agents, myself included, would do a "desk job" in the Chief's office during the early hours of the morning.

Now if you have any concerns about Internal Affairs doing "desk jobs," the thinking, at that time at least, was that at all government offices were for business, and employees should not be keeping documents of a personal nature in their desks. Only matters of official business should be in those desks and any evidence of a criminal nature found in those government desks could be used in a potential criminal case.

So the three of us flew from New York to Boston early one evening, waited until the cleaning people were through with their work at the Federal Building in Boston to do a desk job. We would then fly back to New York.

At about 1:00 AM we entered the office of the Chief of CID and went to work. One of us (not me) was selected to do the job because of his uncanny ability to open just about any lock. He was a good "safe man" but of course one of the good guys.

A search of the desks in the Chief's office failed to disclose anything to indicate any wrongdoing. Meanwhile, our safe expert, having tried

78

about every combination he could think of, couldn't get the damned office safe open. Daylight was beginning to show over Boston Harbor and we were fast running out of time. Finally, in searching the secretary's desk, I stumbled onto her date of birth. Our safe man tried that as a combination and it worked! However, after gaining entrance to the safe, nothing material was found and the Chief was cleared without ever knowing he had been under investigation. Relationship between CID and Internal Affairs remained healthy.

By this time in my career, I had spent 16 years on the street and although I was still enjoying it very much, I had not yet achieved my goal of getting into management. In fact I hoped to end up in higher management before it was all over. But suddenly my days on the street were over, for a while at least. Our New York office was a major one. We had eight squads of eight Special Agents each to cover New York City and Long Island and criminal cases were abundant. Our Assistant Commissioner in Washington, D.C., Mike Acree, was not only a very strong leader but a terrific guy. He was trying hard to push his theory of cross-pollination. That is he tried to encourage mobility within the organization. In fact a couple of years previously, he asked every Special Agent to personally furnish him with his or her current mobility status. I think Audrey and I wrote three drafts before I submitted mine. Mike felt that Special Agents in New York City, with all their experience, could benefit other offices across the country.

But New Yorkers, like Bostonians, were not very mobile. They knew that west of the Hudson River was New Jersey or so they heard. Beyond New Jersey was the rest of the United States but that had very little impact on their lives. East was New England but that was considered to be "the sticks." New Yorkers were content to remain in New York and enjoy their exciting city, despite all its problems.

All except one that is. The Squad Chief or Group Supervisor of Group 4 had accepted a position of Special Agent in Charge of our major office in Florida and I was selected as his replacement. I had finally made it into management.

Although a very gregarious guy and a delight to be around, the prior supervisor of Group 4 seemed to have managed by the seat of his pants. Cases got made but how I was not sure. I found the squad to be in somewhat of a disarray and I had my hands full. Like all new first line managers, the biggest hurdle I had to overcome was that now I could no longer get things done by my own achievement but had to get them done through other people. The concept of "If you want it done right, do it yourself' was no longer available to me. I also had to learn to delegate and this was hard for me. Some people are motivated and some are not. Some are extremely competent at what they do and some don't do quite as well. As a manager, I learned that everyone has a talent for something. One just had to find out where people could contribute.

But in Group 4 I had been blessed with eight Special Agents who were all very competent and motivated investigators. They were not only a good group but a great bunch of guys. (I had no female Special Agents in my group.) I have always believed that management by enthusiasm is the key to success. If the boss doesn't care, his or her subordinates will not care either.

At least enthusiasm was contagious here as these guys ran me ragged. And I mean just that. Although at that time, supervisors were not entitled to overtime, these guys kept me so busy I seldom arrived home before 8:00 PM or 9:00 PM. But I loved it! We had a great squad and the morale was high. I was even able to get a little street time in with them on their cases. After all, how can a manager effectively evaluate people without knowing what they do on the street? Right? Well that was my excuse anyway and my people seemed to enjoy my interest. We had some very successful cases. When an IRS employee called me to report a possible bribery overture it wasn't uncommon to see two or three of my people hanging around the elevators to greet the employee and maybe pick up another possible prosecution case.

But as they say, "All good things come to an end." In January of 1971, Internal Affairs' ten state Western Region based in San Francisco had management problems. Their chief had been the victim of terminal cancer and his Executive Assistant or second in command had left to accept an opportunity elsewhere. A new chief, Joe Dvorak, the Executive Assistant in our Cincinnati office had been selected for the chiefs position In San Francisco and was looking for a new Exec. So two other New York based first line supervisors and I were summoned to Washington, D.C for Oral Board interviews. In those days you were never asked about your current mobility until you appeared at the Oral Board.

At the Oral Board, one supervisor said he was not currently mobile and declined further consideration. The other supervisor, Tony Rizzo, a native New Yorker from Brooklyn and single, was not especially liked by his peers but for some reason was well thought of by some of our higher management. He not only declared his interest but felt he had a lock on the job. In fact after the Oral Board where we were informed a decision would soon be forthcoming, the three of us flew back to New York together. Tony voiced that his only concern was how he could fit his skis on his small sports car when making the trip to San Francisco. He was that confident.

My Oral Board interview seemed to have gone on forever as the newly appointed chief from Cincinnati questioned me thoroughly with respect to my opinions on several management issues and techniques. After 16 years on the street, I had a number of views as to how I would operate as second in command of our Western Region, if selected. Between Tony's confidence about being selected and my reflection on how I did at my Oral Board interview, I flew back to New York thinking I had blown it. As I've said before, "The best speech you make is the one on the way home to yourself."

So by the time I headed back to my New York office the next morning, I had dismissed any chance of being the new Exec in San Francisco and was busy planning my day as supervisor of Group 4. When I got off the elevator at the office, Special Agent Teddy Medwig was getting a drink from the water cooler. He looked up and said, "Congratulations." I said, "Forget it, Teddy. Tony's the one you want to congratulate." He replied, "I don't know. All I know is that late yesterday afternoon, someone called here requesting your social security number." I shrugged and thought to myself that it probably had something to do with the paperwork generated by our Oral Board interviews.

The day started like many others. As I mentioned, the New York Office had eight squads of eight Special Agents each. Each squad had its own squad room including a glassed-in office for the supervisor. I entered our squad room, said my usual good mornings and reached for my in-box as I had been gone almost two days.

About mid-morning I was summoned to the chief's office and advised I had been selected as the new Executive Assistant for the Western Region. I was flabbergasted. I decided I would not call Audrey but would wait to tell her personally that night. I returned to my office, gathered my troops and shared my good news. You could hear a pin drop. They just smiled and returned to their desks. I was a bit confused if not disappointed and went back to my office. About an hour later they all trudged into my office and apologized for not congratulating me earlier. They explained while they were happy for me they felt we had the best squad in the whole New York office and now it would be gone. I was flattered. I told them they would simply get another supervisor but I got the impression they didn't buy into that little speech. Later in my career, when I would meet one of them, we would reflect on what a great squad we had and each would remark that it never remained the same. What an ego builder for me. They were a great bunch of guys.

That evening, Audrey met me at the train station in Ridgewood, N.J. for the short ride home As I hopped in the car she casually asked, "Did they announce the job in San Francisco yet?" I said, "Yep." She said, "Tony Rizzo. Right?" I said, "Nope." She replied, "Then who got the job?" and I grinned and said, "Welcome to San Francisco." She was elated.

Later that evening after dinner, we started making our plans. San Francisco was about 3,000 miles from New York. I had been there once on a rather sensitive case involving Congressional interest for a few days a couple of years previous, but that had been our only exposure to the nation's West Coast. The Western Region wanted me to report for my new assignment in a couple of weeks. This was in January and Audrey and I both knew it would be unwise to pull our three kids out of school in the middle of the school year and expose them to a whole new world right now. We both knew what was coming. Another long separation where Audrey would again be on her own, coping with three kids in a strange city. (We'd only been in Ridgewood for three years.)

EIGHTEEN

Two weeks later I flew to San Francisco and reported for duty. The ten state Western Region, including Alaska and Hawaii, geographically represented about 25% of the land mass in The United States It was a whole new world to me. We had five squads of Special Agents located in San Francisco, Fresno, Ogden, Utah and a major office in Los Angeles with a Special Agent in Charge whose grade was the same grade as my new GS-14. My new chief, Joe Dvorak, although a very dedicated and moral person (maybe to a fault) was a nice guy but he'd had very little criminal investigative experience under his belt. He knew our manual and guidelines backward and forward, but was to depend on me to manage our criminal investigations. The problem was there weren't any, or at least very few. Our major office in Los Angeles had not made a significant criminal case in years and it worried me that public corruption attempts apparently were being ignored. Very few possible bribery overtures were being reported.

I began to settle in with my new role as Executive Assistant but Audrey and the kids were still 3,000 miles away. I was living in a hotel room on Nob Hill. I will say that if a married man is stuck somewhere away from home for four months, San Francisco is a pretty nice place to be. I hate to use the word charming because it sounds somewhat effeminate to me but that's what that city is. But Joe Dvorak was a very demanding chief who worked long hours and expected and got the same from me. I averaged at least ten hours a day but we had a lot of work ahead of us and there was much to do. On weekends, I would walk the Golden Gate Bridge, an exhilarating experience that I would highly recommend. Afterward I often ate at the Army's Presidio's PX which I also enjoyed.

About two months after reporting to San Francisco, a major case evolved. Someone had threatened the life of "Lettuce King" Caesar Chavez, head of the Migrant Workers' Union. ATF had the investigation. During that investigation, several allegations of ATF misconduct surfaced and our Director of Internal Affairs, who was my former chief in New York, decreed that I was to personally supervise our case. Unfortunately the timing was bad because after two months away from home, I had finally received permission to get back there for a few days. I had purchased my airline tickets and had just returned from the airline terminal where I had forwarded my luggage when Dvorak received the call from our director. Joe informed me I had to cancel my trip home because the director had assigned me to boss the Caesar Chavez case. I pleaded with Joe, pointing out that my luggage was already on its way to New Jersey but all I got out of him was, "Sorry, George. That's the job." He finally allowed me to call our director personally who laughed and said, "Go home, George. Caesar Chavez will still be there when you get back." Ironically, Joe had discovered the same manual regulations that allowed me a brief trip home and he too took advantage of it and went back to Cincinnati for a few days.

Our director had been right. When I returned to San Francisco, the Chavez case was waiting for me and I spent 10 to 12 hours a day plus weekends on it. The result was the threats on the life of Chavez ceased but several ATF Special Agents received disciplinary action, two were removed from office and a top ATF official in the Western Region was transferred to Washington, D.C. That one, I thought was very unfair as his only sin had been to trust one of his subordinate chiefs. But that's the federal government for you. Someone had to pay. But no one ever said life was fair. Right?

After being away from Audrey and the kids for four months, school was out and I finally returned to Ridgewood to arrange for our big move. We sold our English Tudor in a remarkable six days and headed off to the West Coast in the family car. We found a nice home in Walnut Creek in Contra Costa County, just outside of San Francisco and settled in to a new life in California.

Our former top managers in the Western region had been gone for some time now and Joe and I had some rebuilding to do. All our personnel were home grown so to speak, and Joe and I were considered outsiders (guys from the east) which certainly didn't help. To make matters worse, those in our major Los Angeles office, looked at our San Francisco Headquarters Office with a "we and they" attitude. I was well aware that my new assignment would be a real challenge.

Another problem was surfacing. It appeared that IRS's Integrity Awareness program had been sadly neglected or at least ineffective. Everyone seemed to think that all the public corruption problems were "back east." Treasury employees were either not reporting bribery attempts or were not recognizing them. We thought that maybe it was because our presentations were being made by Special Agents who had no experience in this area. Well all of that had come to a screeching halt now as Joe no longer trusted our local Special Agents to make Integrity Awareness presentations. He informed me that from now on, in addition to my other responsibilities as second in command, I was to make all theses presentations personally. This may have been flattering but it was an awesome task. Just about every two weeks I found myself traveling the 500 miles from San Francisco to Los Angeles and back. Other presentations were in

Fresno, Seattle, Portland, Oregon, Boise, Idaho, and Helena, Montana, among other cities. There was a lot of travel involved. Once I had five Integrity Awareness presentations in Las Vegas and Reno, Nevada within two days. I was getting sick of listening to myself.

But it seemed we were reaching them. A month after I made a presentation in Fresno, a Revenue Agent stationed there reported what he thought might be a bribery overture. It seemed that he had a doctor under audit who owed an additional $50,000 in tax liability. The doctor, an M.D. when told of the sad news had asked the Revenue Agent, "Can't we work this out somehow to our mutual advantage?" Bingo! A possible bribe overture. Since our Special Agents in Fresno had never worked an attempted bribery case, guess who ended up supervising it. Right. Lonesome George. But I was in my own element.

As always, we wired up the Revenue Agent who really was a sharp guy. He met with the good doctor who again made the same offer. At a subsequent meeting, he paid the Revenue Agent $10,000 in cash to eliminate his substantial tax liability. He was subsequently indicted and I'll never forget that indictment. The Assistant U.S. Attorney responsible for the Grand Jury had previously heard our tape recordings of the conversations between the Revenue Agent and the doctor and had decided that the Grand Jury should hear them. As I was in the Grand Jury room setting up the tape recorder for them, I heard the Assistant U.S. Attorney tell them, "Now here's how we're gonna indict this guy." I thought to myself, "I guess I don't have to worry about this indictment." So if anyone has any doubt about the role of the Government's attorney in a Grand Jury, believe me, he or she points them in the right direction. But remember, the role of a Grand Jury is not to decide the fate of a potential defendant. All that is needed for an indictment is probable cause to believe that a person might have committed the alleged crime involved.

As I mentioned previously, among many other Integrity Awareness presentations I had made, I'd had three in Las Vegas and two in Reno in a two-day period. The experience had been very demanding but boy, did it ever pay off. Big time! About two months after I had made these presentations, a Las Vegas based Revenue Agent called to report that he had an individual under audit who, we will refer to as Lenny Crutchwood. Crutchwood ran an auto rental agency out of a booth located in one of the casinos on The Strip in Las Vegas and it was rumored that he was on the peripheral of organized crime. He had offered the Revenue Agent $1,500 to wipe out his tax.

After hearing about the Revenue Agent's call, my chief said, "George, I want you to personally supervise this one, no matter how long it takes. Don't worry. I'll take care of things here in San Francisco." I thought, "Yeah, I bet you will." So off I went to Las Vegas with two Special Agents from our Los Angeles office. The offer had been very direct so I briefed the Revenue Agent that after he had received the money, he should ask Crutchwood if he knew of anyone else who might need some help with their tax problems. He did so and later Crutchwood called him and asked the Revenue Agent to meet with him to which he agreed. Of course we monitored that meeting and it was a shocker.

Crutchwood indicated that he had two friends who were co-owners of a major casino on The Strip who were under audit by the IRS and it appeared they would owe a substantial amount of money. We knew it was rumored that this casino might have strong organized crime connections. The Revenue Agent properly advised Crutchwood that he would see what he could do and get back to him.

But after the meeting, the Revenue Agent came to me and looked a little nervous. He said he wanted no further part of this case. He also said he had looked at the audit history of this casino and it appeared that the co-owners might be referred to IRS's Criminal Investigation Division for tax evasion.

That seemed to resolve the problem we had with a reluctant Revenue Agent who we certainly didn't want to put pressure on. If we could find a CID Special Agent who was willing to take our case further, we'd be okay. And we did. Luckily we found a gung ho guy whom we will refer to as Bill Crampton who agreed to be assigned to CID's potential criminal case and go from there. He arranged to meet with one of the casino's co-owners who was very concerned about his tax problems. In keeping with CID's policy, he was read his rights and although he was trying to feel out the Special Agent, no direct overtures were forthcoming at first. But at subsequent meetings, all covered by Internal Affairs of course, he started to make vague references about how to resolve the tax problems so that all parties would be satisfied. The Special Agent handled himself well, especially when the casino's co-owner suggested they have a serious conversation in the casino's sauna. Crampton reluctantly agreed. Now this presented us with certain technical difficulties. There is only one place on a nude body where we could place a monitoring device without it being seen and Crampton declined that one. We certainly couldn't blame him. We were not especially concerned about Crampton's safety as he was a federal criminal investigator and the chances of his being hurt or worse in a casino sauna were almost nil. So the sauna meeting was not monitored or recorded.

After his meeting with the casino's co-owner in the sauna, Crampton met with us and advised the co-owner had made his pitch. He offered Crampton $50,000 personally in cash, if Crampton would recommend against criminal prosecution for tax evasion.

In subsequent conversations which were recorded by Internal Affairs, the casino's co-owner repeated the $50,000 bribe offer to Crampton and eventually he was given $50,000 in cash in a suit case. The money was logged into evidence and three arrests were made, the two co-owners and of course Lenny Crutchwood. Naturally, it hit the front page headlines of the Las Vegas newspaper as at the time it was the biggest bribe offer in the history of the Internal Revenue Service. The Western Region was riding high. Our people in New York couldn't believe it. New York was where it was all about. Or was it? I held on to a copy of those headlines and I'm glad I did as they later played a significant part of my future career. The CID Special Agent was given significant recognition as well.

NINETEEN

Well it looked like the Western Region was finally coming to age. A lot of our older Special Agents apparently felt that all this heavy street stuff was a little too much for them and some retired or went to another agency. In addition, our national office in Washington, D.C. realizing the vast terrain that Western Region covered, allotted us five new positions, so we had quite a few Special Agent slots open now. As a result, I got into the hiring business which I've always enjoyed. In one week I interviewed candidates in Los Angeles, San Diego, Portland, Oregon, and Seattle Washington. But my trip was successful and we ended up with five new Special Agents who turned out to be good employees.

But the hiring of new employees creates a real training problem. Although like all other new U.S. Treasury Agents, our new people were required to attend the Treasury Law Enforcement Training Center in Glenco, Georgia, for two months, a very intensive but excellent course. The rest was up to us. I'm afraid they ended up with a crash course in street experience as they were put into situations they may not have been ready for. That's a tough way to learn in law enforcement but one certainly learns fast in this business and most of our people reacted well.

Our Special Agent in Charge in Los Angeles really didn't get along that well with our new chief and I think the feeling was mutual. He was a gentleman and a real nice guy but had been in that position for some time now and felt that enough was enough. Our caseload in San Diego, about 100 miles south of Los Angeles had increased significantly and we had decided to open up a one Special Agent office there. He didn't live that far away from San Diego and even though it meant a reduction in salary, he applied for the job and was selected. He did a fine job there for us.

But that created a vacancy for his former position in Los Angeles and guess who got selected for that? My old competitor, Tony Rizzo from New York. When I heard that news, I called our director in Washington, D.C. I said, "I understand Tony Rizzo is our new Special Agent in Charge in Los Angeles." He replied, "Yeah. He'll be there shortly." I said, "What did I ever do to you to deserve that?" The director just laughed and said "Believe me, George, I had nothing to do with that one but don't worry. You'll survive." I guess I did as Tony and I, never really close, ended up in a peaceful co-existence.

While in the Western Region, I made my television debut, if you can call it a debut that is. The Commissioner of Internal Revenue Service had been invited to appear as guest speaker at a CPA luncheon in San Francisco and we were asked to provide a protection detail, I had a Special Agent pick him up at the airport and transport him to the hotel where the luncheon was to be held, without incident. Then our chief came into my office and said, "George, I certainly don't want anything to happen to the Commissioner while he is visiting San Francisco. I want you to head up a three Special Agent detail to provide protection of the Commissioner at that CPA luncheon. So we headed for the hotel and set up outside the conference room where the luncheon was to be held.

As soon as the attendees arrived, we secured the doors and it was a good thing we did as about 15 minutes later some 20 tax protestors showed up with all their signs, followed, of course, by three network reporters and camera people. The tax protestors seemed to be represented by some guy ranting and raving about our tax system. We barred them from the entrance, pointing out that it was a private luncheon. Then the leader of the group got into my face yelling about his constitutional rights, freedom of speech and the right to protest. Of course the television cameras and microphones were up there too. Not known for my patience or abundance of diplomacy, I finally gave the protesters their marching orders. Three San Francisco officers were there, too but just sat around offering us no help at all which really pissed me off. Finally everything calmed down.

That night, when I got home, Audrey and I were watching the evening news on television. The station we were watching had captured a close-up of me yelling into the protest leader's face, "I don't care what you say. You're not going in there." Audrey then yelled to our son who was in his bedroom, "Steve, Dad's on TV." He came out, looked and said, "Looks like a new sport jacket you've got on, Dad. I haven't seen that one before." So much for impressing your kids. Right? .

Audrey and I both knew that we were not going to spend the rest of our days in California. While we enjoyed it there, she often commented,

"It's nice here but it's too far from everything." I took that to mean too far from Cape Cod or Maine. I had no special desire to relocate back to New England as I'd had enough snow and cold weather to last me a lifetime. But I did want to end up my career with U.S. Treasury as a chief somewhere. After three years in the Western Region, the chief's job in the eight state Southwest Region headquartered in Dallas opened up. My old friend Jim Quinn, the chief there, had a son who was a gifted athlete and was playing football for Penn. State. Jim wanted to thoroughly enjoy his son's success and requested a lateral transfer to Washington, D.C. to be closer. His request had been granted and now the chief's job in the Southwest Region was open. Both Tony Rizzo and I put in for it and once again, I got the job.

TWENTY

In September of 1974 we relocated to Dallas and found a beautiful home within seven miles of my new office. We had heard elsewhere that Texans were a bit overbearing and bragged a lot about their state. We found them to be the friendliest people we had even been exposed to. They simply loved their state and had a dedication to it that we considered admirable. Nice people.

If there is one thing I've learned in life it is that a change of scenery does not automatically eliminate your problems. You just get a new set of them and upon my arrival in Dallas, I found some big ones. Our eight state Southwest Region had about 65 Special Agents with offices in Dallas, Austin, Houston, New Orleans, Denver, Oklahoma City and Wichita, Kansas. We later opened offices in Little Rock and San Antonio. A lot of our personnel were old timers and they'd had very few prosecution cases. In fact, the year I reported for duty they'd had only three. Sound familiar? Pretty sad, I thought. I found that three out of our four supervisors were not supervising at all. They were not pushing for good criminal cases and failed to generate any enthusiasm whatsoever. The fourth supervisor, Bob Gorham was doing a good job but we had just promoted him as my new Exec. Of the three remaining, one retired, one was a nice guy but I felt had no supervisory skills so I reassigned him to other duties at the same salary and he was happy. The remaining supervisor we will talk about later. It was clearly the "good old boy" syndrome bumping along and Jim Quinn had only been chief here for two years. His second in command, who had recently retired, had little criminal investigative experience. Jim had little opportunity to make any significant impact.

Bob Gorham, my new Executive Assistant or second in command, had set up our annual seminar just about the time I had reported for duty and it was an ideal time for me to meet my new troops. It was also a good time for them to get their first look at their new chief. After being introduced, I addressed our new people. I told them of the goals I had envisioned and answered their questions as best I could. I then dragged out my news clip on the $50,000 bribe case in Las Vegas, all framed. I told them that this was the type of case and headlines I wanted to see in the Southwest Region. I said I knew they could do it. They all smiled at me but I couldn't really tell if I had reached them.

The next two or three years were rough. Three of the supervisors were replaced with Bill Sullivan from Boston, Marty Ilaqua from Cincinnati and Roy Moran a former Virginia State Trooper stationed in Washington, D.C. The fourth supervisor, I had mentioned earlier, turned out to be a big problem. He had about eight Special Agents with an office about 200 miles from our Dallas headquarters and it seemed one of them had gone around the bend and desperately needed psychological help. The situation had so deteriorated that other Special Agents refused to work with him and he had become a serious safety hazard. But the supervisor was protecting him and had never informed me or Bob Gorham of the situation. Finally, while I was on a visitation to that office, two Special Agents who had my confidence alerted me to the situation. The Special Agent with the mental problem was given a disability retirement and the supervisor retired. Thank heaven he was eligible. He was replaced with a homegrown guy who did a good job and we were finally able to get some good cases going there.

The other Special Agents who, and I like to use the phrase, "couldn't find a crime in a phone booth" either retired or went to another agency. They simply weren't doing what they were being paid to do and I had little sympathy for them. This of course presented me with the same challenge I'd had in the Western Region. Once again I became personally involved in searching for new people I thought might do well with our organization.

Looking across the country at my counterparts, it seemed that most chiefs were delegating the responsibility of hiring new people to their first line managers. Then if that person did not live up to the expectations required, the chief had an out. He hadn't personally hired the person. I had strong feelings in this area. I felt that I should take the full responsibility for hiring new people and for any mistakes or misjudgment made in the process. However, I did take the first line manager with me on interviews whenever possible. So I started my search. I traveled as far north as Fargo, South Dakota, west to Salt Lake City, east to Boston and as far south as Miami. I'd been able to develop almost a profile of what made a good Special Agent. I can recall a supervisor I had known in Newark, New Jersey saying, "If you want a good employee, hire one coming from a lousy agency. They are far more motivated." He was right. I ended up with a lot of young men and women who had Bachelor degrees in Criminal Justice a degree of some sort, or had prior law enforcement experience or both.

I got into a big contest with Washington, D.C. as they did not want to pick up any moving expenses for the new hires. But I couldn't see how we could expect someone being hired as grade GS-5, which was a little over the poverty level, to relocate across the country on his/her own. I finally won and relocation expenses were eventually paid.

But as I've said before, when hiring new people, training problems are inevitable and we had a lot of training to do if we were ever going to put the Southwest Region on the map, so to speak. Of course they were all required to attend the previously mentioned Federal Law Enforcement Training Center in Glenco, Georgia, for the required two months and that provided them with basic law enforcement skills including firearms training, interview techniques, surveillance and, federal criminal law. The rest of their training would be provided on the job with more experienced Special Agents. There weren't that many that fit that category.

TWENTY-ONE

Internal Affairs had recently been given an additional responsibility and a very important one. The IRS Assault Program. The threat of assault on IRS employees was increasing nationwide, particularly in the southwest and northwest areas. Nobody likes to see an IRS employee show up at his door looking for delinquent taxes. Revenue Officers responsible for this difficult task are not federal law enforcement officers. They are merely tax collectors with no authority to arrest or enforce the federal criminal law. Often they seek people who might be in a financial crunch at the time and when a Revenue Officer shows up, they threaten him or worse. He gets assaulted. A few of these people simply don't want to pay their taxes. Some folks have negative feelings about the federal government, especially the IRS. Some people, especially those living in the sparsely settled areas of the country, with their cultural background and where the "Old West" still prevails, can be quite hostile. Statements like, "If you come back here again, I'll blow your head off" are made? Occasionally they will actually assault an IRS employee who is simply trying to do his job. (An assault on a female employee was always rare.)

The IRS's Assault Program had previously been the responsibility of their Criminal Investigation Division but they were not particularly comfortable with the priority CID was giving it. It was thought that if the program was given to Internal Affairs to enforce, it might produce a better rapport between IRS and Internal Affairs who also had the responsibility of conducting criminal misconduct investigations on IRS employees.

As I indicated previously, most threats against IRS employees on behalf of the taxpayer (or non-taxpayer) were idle threats brought about by mere frustration. In those cases two of our Special Agents would call on the person making the threat and advise him (it was usually a male) that it was against the federal law to threaten a public official and further occurrence might result in an arrest and subsequent prosecution. This usually worked and many times the person apologized. At least we got his attention. If an actual assault occurred, we would get an arrest warrant and arrest the individual.

Where isolated areas were concerned, we would usually send just one Special Agent and he or she would pick up a local officer or a U.S. Marshall for a backup. Sometimes this didn't work so well as when we asked local officers for a backup, we'd get a reply like, "Are you kidding? We're not going anywhere near that guy. He's a nut."

But generally our policy with respect to the IRS Assault Program was working. We were not always thrilled with the policy of the U.S. Attorney's Office in some areas and it was a drain on our limited resources, but it did result in a much better rapport with the IRS employee population and a greater understanding of our mission to insure the integrity of U.S. Treasury.

TWENTY-TWO

In the early 70's various right wing groups broke out across the western and northwestern parts of the United States. They called themselves The Posse Comitatus. Although Webster's Dictionary defines Posse Comitatus as "any body of persons with legal authority," these people recognized only the sheriff as having legal authority. They did not recognize local authority or federal authority, including the FBI. They had especially not recognized IRS and its authority to collect income tax. Many of these groups were armed and holding combat training sessions. We were especially concerned about the safety of Treasury employees attempting to conduct audits and collect delinquent taxes. Internal Affairs Special Agents had to be ready at any given time to respond to threats made by Posse Comitatus groups. To make matters worse, at that time we were restricted from collecting any intelligence information on those groups, among others, which didn't help any. Because of the potential danger to our Special Agents, I chose to ignore this policy and although intelligence information was collected, one could not find any evidence of it in our files, if you get my drift.

As Chief, I was expected to visit our four major offices at least once a month and I did. On one occasion, I was to visit our office in Denver at a time when a Posse Comitatus group was kicking up its heels in the neighboring state of Wyoming. So that meant that I had to carry my issued weapon with me. That evening I checked into my hotel in Denver and spent a peaceful evening there.

The following morning, anticipating a very busy day, I checked my weapon into the office safe and went out for an early breakfast. Although not in an especially great neighborhood, I entered a respectable restaurant and ordered my bacon and eggs. Just as the meal was set in front of me at a table, I saw trouble walk in the door. After all these years in our business, one can just smell trouble and this guy coming in the door looked like bad news. I was convinced he was about to hold the place up. He looked at the manager who seemed to be a little nervous as well and then looked at me. Terrific! My weapon was in the office safe and the only defense I had was a plate of bacon and eggs, which I was about to throw at him should he approach me first. Then two uniformed Denver police officers walked in the door. The guy took one look at them and split. My breakfast sure hit the spot and we had no trouble with the Posse Comitatus during my visit.

I had been a Chief in the Southwest region for three years now and we were getting into pretty good shape. Bob Gorham, my Exec and I were very compatible, if not good friends, and our people, for the most part relatively new, were getting valuable street experience and loving it. Enthusiasm was high and good criminal cases were being made. As Chief, I continued to be active in our Integrity Awareness programs even though it meant extra travel.

One problem we had was a weaponry problem. Nationwide, our Internal Affairs Special Agents were carrying antiquated Colt revolvers. Wheel guns. I had no problem with wheel guns but these must have been issued under the Abraham Lincoln administration and I continued to grind away at our National Office to get us some decent weapons. I always got the same answer. No money for guns was the reply from civilians who controlled the purse strings and who could not relate to law enforcement needs. So I finally took some action on my own. I told the members of our Dallas based group to discretely inquire whether ATF had seized any weapons they could spare.

Then one afternoon I was looking out my first floor office window and saw four of my people approaching the office, dragging some heavy bags which looked like they weighed a ton. They then entered my office grinning from ear to ear. They had collected about 80 seized weapons from ATF. One Special Agent said, "We think we got what you wanted, Chief." So we sorted the weapons out, gave the unacceptable ones back to ATF and issued new weapons to all our people in the Southwest Region. Of course, we had to send the old weapons back to Washington, D.C. and that lit the fuse. I was told that I had set our weaponry program (if there ever was one) back years and that my counterparts across the country would be furious. I apologized and said I would not do it again, but of course, they knew I would. It seemed the other chiefs across the country were more envious than disturbed. Morale soared in the Southwest Region as my people knew I really cared.

TWENTY-THREE

Then our Integrity Awareness program started to pay off. Big time! One of IRS' CID Special Agents stationed at their Fort Worth office called to report a bribe overture from a bookmaker he had under investigation. This was somewhat unusual as any subject of a CID investigation was immediately given his or her Miranda Rights at the first CID contact. That usually intimidates people and discourages bribe overtures but I guess this guy just didn't want to go to the federal penitentiary.

As always, we did our thing and wired up the Special Agent who again met with the bookmaker and the bribe offer was repeated. It was kind of shaky at first as the bookmaker appeared a little nervous about paying off a federal law enforcement officer but eventually he gave him $2,000 to kill his tax evasion case. Of course we now had it all on tape eliminating any future defense of entrapment.

Per our instructions, after the money went down, the CID Special Agent asked the bookmaker whether he knew any people in his business who were in trouble with IRS and needed help. The bookmaker said he would put out the word and did. Naturally he was not arrested at the time. The case dragged on for over a year and we ended up with not one or two or five but ten bookmakers in the Dallas Fort Worth metroplex who met with the CID Special Agent and paid him various amounts of money to have their criminal investigations killed.

The Internal Affairs Special Agent coordinating this big case had been one of my new hires and I was as proud as a new father. He was doing a terrific job. I privately gave him a few pointers along the way but I carefully let him build his confidence and the admiration of his peers. I found no jealousy but just the opposite. I found pride and admiration. The Southwest Region had finally made a big case.

I decided that for greater impact, we would arrest all ten bookmakers on the same day. We chose a Sunday when we could probably find most of them at home. All of our Special Agents in the other five offices participated in the roundup and all ten bookmakers were arrested the same day. Of course old Lonesome George was right there on sight in the middle of it all and not one horror story came out of all ten arrests. We made the headlines of both the Dallas Morning News and the Fort Worth Telegram. The Southwest region had finally come of age and I can tell you, I was one proud chief.

TWENTY-FOUR

Even though the big case in the Dallas Fort Worth area had been a success with ten bookmakers being convicted of attempting to bribe a public official, I was still worried about New Orleans. For years New Orleans had the reputation for public corruption and whether it was justified or not, I was concerned that it might have impact on our Treasury employees there. My predecessor, Jim Quinn, had also recognized this. Jim had talked a Special Agent from New York whom we both knew, into a lateral transfer to New Orleans in an attempt to identify public corruption there as it impacted our Treasury employees. This Special Agent, although having achieved much success in the stock market, reaching millionaire status at one point, had not had that much success on the job in New York. I personally had attributed this to his poor attitude toward management. At any rate, he had been given free reign to develop cases in New Orleans without struggling with an assigned caseload for two or three years now and we still didn't have a handle on possible corruption there. So I met with him in New Orleans and told him we could no longer justify his position in New Orleans and would have to transfer him to Houston where his services could be better utilized. He decided not to transfer there and retired. That created a vacancy for a grade GS-12 Special Agent's position in New Orleans.

I decided to go nationwide within Internal Affairs in search of someone I thought could develop good intelligence information and cases in New Orleans. In doing so I found a Special Agent at the Midwest Region's post of duty in Milwaukee who expressed an interest. His name was Howard Shuster and although he was very much a country boy, somehow he impressed me as someone with good potential and I hired him. It was probably one of the best management decisions I ever made.

Immediately after reporting for duty in New Orleans, Howard established rapport with all the other federal law enforcement agencies in the New Orleans area, including FBI, which developed into a very positive move for us. Howard was assigned cases and he worked with enthusiasm. He developed a confidential informant who alleged that a Revenue Officer in IRS responsible for collecting delinquent taxes was "on the take."

At the time, the FBI had leased a small office over a restaurant in New Orleans for a sting operation which had just concluded. Since the lease was still in effect, Howard asked if we could use that office for a couple of weeks and they generously agreed. So in an effort to determine whether or not the allegation was true that we had a corrupt Revenue Officer, we set up an operation there.

We had a first line manager in Austin who, before getting into law enforcement had obtained a degree in drama if you will. Perfect for us. His name was John Gibson. We set John up in our borrowed office in an undercover capacity. He posed as a small businessman from Baltimore who had just relocated to New Orleans when business in Baltimore had dropped off. Supposedly, John had substantial tax delinquency accounts and could not afford to pay them off at the time. Gibson had just returned from vacation and was sporting a beard which was a no-no in the Southwest Region. Coming from a spit and polish outfit like the Massachusetts State Police, I didn't feel beards were appropriate for federal law enforcement officers and although our dress code did not forbid them, my people knew my feelings and we had no beards. But I felt we had an exception here and John was allowed to keep it for a bit.

Surreptitiously we had someone contact the Revenue officer and give him the address of John's newly acquired office and an appointment was set up. We videotaped the conversation between John and the Revenue Officer and John played his role perfectly. He told the Revenue Officer of his tax problems in Baltimore and asked if the Revenue Officer had any suggestions as to how he could settle them. The Revenue Officer said he would immediately have John's tax delinquency accounts transferred to New Orleans and be assigned to him. He said he would then place them in an inactive status saying that the taxpayer was unable to pay at this time. John appeared delighted and asked the Revenue Officer how much it would cost. The Revenue Officer replied, "Three hundred dollars" which we thought was cheap. Can you imagine a government employee in a position of trust selling his integrity for $300? But he did.

After the Revenue Officer had taken the $300 bribe, John mentioned that since he was new to the New Orleans area, he would need a new accountant. He asked the Revenue Officer if he knew anyone who knew his way around IRS and the Revenue Officer said he knew just the right guy. He added that John could expect a call from someone real soon.

Within a day or so the accountant telephoned John at our temporary office and always anxious to find a new client, showed up. He spent about 45 minutes with John, showing John how John could effectively cheat on his taxes with very little chance of being caught. Incidentally the accountant was not a CPA. Of course we videotaped this conversation too.

The case concluded with the Revenue Officer, being convicted as a corrupt public official, went to the federal penitentiary and the accountant was barred from representing clients before IRS. In addition, using the videotapes between John and the Revenue Officer and John and the accountant, we were able to produce training tapes to be used at Integrity Awareness presentations to all IRS field people, nationwide.

TWENTY-FIVE

Shortly after out big case in New Orleans concluded, our NORP Team showed up. By way of explanation, our NORP Team was made up of members of the National Office Review Program. All participants were assigned to our National Office in Washington, D.C., most of whom, in my opinion, couldn't make it in the field. Every year or so a NORP Team visited all our field offices to review operations, closed cases, records keeping, communications, morale and local management policy. Of course you know everyone in the field looked forward to that but maybe it did serve a purpose. It kept a few managers from getting a little sloppy.

I was given a very good report card, if you will. We had good personnel, good cases and morale was high. I found their rationale rather ironic because a couple of years after I had become Chief of the Southwest Region, I was told we had a huge training problem. No kidding! With all the new Special Agents we hired, of course we did and had addressed that problem. That particular NORP Team also told me we had a big morale problem. I disagreed. Their conclusion had been based upon their interviews with former Special Agents that I had chased out the door. Naturally, they wouldn't make any positive remarks. So now the NORP Team advised me that the morale problem (which we never had) had been resolved and morale was now high. In fact I was lauded for the people we now had. In recognition for my accomplishments I was given a rather left handed compliment, at least in my mind. I was detailed into our National Office as Acting Assistant Director of Internal Affairs for three months. The rationale was that I might make a similar contribution, nationwide.

So off I went to Washington, D.C. I'm sure Audrey wondered if it would all ever end. But at least the kids had grown up by then and she had found a job with a local insurance company which she enjoyed.

I found an apartment complex in Georgetown named "The Intrigue." Audrey wasn't especially thrilled with the name but it was very comfortable and fairly handy to our Washington, D.C. office. I was allowed to fly home every other weekend which I thought was rather generous and the weekends I was there I enjoyed all the museums and other impressive attractions our seat of government offers to this great country of ours. Meanwhile the Southwest Region continued to bump along, still making good cases, but I was still anxious to get home again for good.

Speaking of good cases. After I had concluded my detail in Washington, D.C., a big case surfaced in Oklahoma City. Special Agent Jack Henry, stationed in IRS's CID in Oklahoma City called to report that the previous day, a Sunday, a small businessman he'd had under investigation for tax fraud for eight months, had called him at home. He thought the taxpayer whom we shall call Howard Kingsley might be making a bribe overture. According to Henry, Kingsley had said, "Let's get together sometime alone and get things settled. I'll take care of you somewhere down the line." Henry commented that Kingsley had previously suggested they go hunting or fishing together sometime but he had ignored the comment. He said that he now anticipated a strong possibility that Kingsley might make a bribe overture.

We then recorded a conversation between Special Agent Henry and Kingsley where Kingsley repeated the comment that they should get together alone and take care of things and he would take care of Henry somewhere down the line. A meeting was set for the next day at an Oklahoma City motel lounge where Henry would return some bank records he had been reviewing. At the time we only had one Special Agent assigned to our Oklahoma City office and we had to hustle to cover that meeting.

Special Agent Henry also mentioned that he and Kingsley had a mutual acquaintance. Henry had investigated someone Kingsley knew and probably Kingsley knew that person had never been prosecuted. He said that shortly thereafter, that person "bumped into" Henry near Henry's office but that the subject of Kingsley or his tax problems never came up. He offered that maybe it had only been a coincidence but the issue was never resolved.

The motel lounge in the hotel where Henry and Kingsley met was on the first floor so we set up our operation in a second floor motel room overlooking it with a video camera and a zoom lens plus audio equipment and covered it from there.

At the meeting Henry told Kingsley that for that particular year it appeared Kingsley had $75,000 in unsubstantiated deductions which would therefore be considered as false. Kingsley was probably aware that the civil penalties assessed would be 50% per year! He said, "What can you do for me, Jack? I'll take care of you down the line. You save me $200,000 and I'll give you 10%." Henry then asked Kingsley to clarify his statement and Kingsley responded, "I have $5,000 cash in my boot right now plus another $1,000 in my pocket. It's all in $100 bills." At that point, there was no question in our minds that the taxpayer was predisposed and his intention was to bribe Special Agent Henry.

In further conversation, Kingsley said that he had paid $84,000 in tax the previous year. Now comfortable that he was talking to a corrupt Special Agent, he asked Henry if he could file an amended tax return for that year and get his money back. He said that if this could be arranged, they would split the money fifty-fifty. Henry said he would look into it. Kingsley then paid Henry $6,000 in cash and a second meeting was set up for within two weeks time.

At their second meeting at the same hotel lounge which we covered with the same setup, Kingsley cautioned Special Agent Henry not to spend his money too fast. Henry said he was well aware of the bank's requirement to report all cash transactions over $10,000 to IRS. Kingsley then again brought up the possibility of filing an amended tax return for the prior year and Henry, per our instructions, said, "It's looking pretty good." Kingsley said, "Good, Jack. I knew you knew what you were doing." He then paid Henry $14,000 money in cash and they left the motel lounge together.

In the parking lot Kingsley was arrested by Internal Affairs Special Agents for Bribery of a Public Official. He was pretty upset with us for that. He claimed we should have arrested him after he'd paid Henry the initial $6,000 so he could have saved $14,000.

The case was then referred to the U.S. Attorney's Office in Oklahoma City and Kingsley was subsequently indicted and prosecuted. With our video- and audiotapes and no defense of entrapment available, he was convicted and sentenced to five years in the federal penitentiary at Big Spring, Texas. Special Agent Henry received the esteemed Commissioner of Internal Revenue Service's Award. We were delighted with Henry's comments about working with Internal Affairs. He said that like most Treasury employees, he considered Internal Affairs Special Agents to be headhunters but after working with them, he felt they were simply protecting his job and his integrity.

Seeing this case as having good potential for another training tape to use in our Integrity Awareness Program, we sought the assistance of IRS's television studio in Arlington, Virginia, that had been so much help in producing our previous tapes. Their television crew came out to Oklahoma City and we taped the scene and an interview with Special Agent Henry. The

Assistant U.S. Attorney who successfully prosecuted Kingsley agreed to a television interview as did the judge who presided over the case. Both did an outstanding job. I was even able to talk Howard Kingsley, now incarcerated at the federal facility in Big Spring, Texas, into an interview. Once again the tape, which we named "The Money Boot," was shown nationally to all IRS field employees and the feedback was very positive. It made the point that Bribery of a Public Official did not just occur in big cities like New York, Los Angeles or Chicago, but even in a mid-sized city like Oklahoma City. Our whole concern was and still is that if attempted bribery overtures are not timely and properly reported to Internal Affairs, that a corrupt taxpayer or his or her representative will continue to make bribery overtures to other employees and might very well succeed. As long as Treasury continues to hire from the human race, some employee with severe financial problems or worse, might be tempted and that would result in serious problems for that employee and damage the reputation of U.S. Treasury and other functions. That is unacceptable to all law abiding citizens who live in the best country in the world.

I had been the chief of our eight state Southwest Region for ten years now and it appeared my clock was running down. We'd come a long way. The year I was appointed we'd had only three prosecution cases. In my tenth year we'd topped the whole country including our major office in New York, with 65 prosecution cases. I was still getting inquiries from my counterparts across the country as to how I had found such talented people. In addition, I was facing the 55-year-old mandatory retirement age for federal officers. It was time to go.

That September we were preparing for our annual seminar and I wanted it to be remembered as something special. It seemed like Vale, Colorado, would be a place everyone would enjoy, including our clerical help. But I knew Washington, D.C. would think it too prestigious and not approve that location. So I chose the town of Frisco, only a few miles away from Vale and they bought it. At that time of the year, Colorado was between the autumn and ski seasons so we ended up with a great hotel at a very reasonable price.

It was there that I announced my intended retirement and everyone was shocked. I never came across as one of those "I'll be glad to get out of here" types. During my ten years in the Southwest region. I'd hired 90% of our staff and we were very close. My retirement party produced a few embarrassing tears from me which I attributed to an allergy I was suffering from. (An allergy in January? Come on, George.) There were about 100 people there including a number of high level officials and I was deeply honored.

TWENTY-SIX

Audrey and I celebrated my retirement with a trip to Europe. I had been considering two opportunities for fairly high positions in law enforcement. One was in Colorado and the other in Massachusetts. Of course that meant relocation and Audrey wanted to be eligible for her retirement at her insurance job. Also, to be quite honest, after 30 years in the business, I was a little tired and chose to finally stop and smell the roses for a bit.

I enjoyed retirement for a while with a lot of golf and catching up to do, but it only lasted two years and I was getting restless. This was not consistent with the life of Lonesome George. One simply cannot run at the pace I'd become accustomed to and suddenly come to a screeching halt. I guess what actually saved me was a murder trial.

Like on all other occasions when I had been selected for jury duty, I had taken my little paperback down to the courthouse, waited patiently all morning until the voir dire was completed and when dismissed, I went home. I knew that no defense attorney in his or her right mind would want me on a jury. It disappointed me a little as with all my years in law enforcement, especially prosecuting my own cases while with Massachusetts State Police, I would have enjoyed the experience of sitting on a jury to see for myself just how justice evolved. But I knew that would never happen.

Oh yeah? Wrong, George! Surprisingly this time I made it through the voir dire and was selected for a murder trial. In fact, after being exposed to many a defense attorney over the years, this one impressed me as very sharp. His defendant had been accused of murdering his ex-wife and for some reason had been granted a second trial. I guess his attorney (court appointed) knew he had a loser and had decided he might be better off with people on the jury who were at least halfway intelligent.

After the prosecution and defense attorneys rested their case and the judge made his charge to the jury, we retired to the jury room and shortly thereafter, returned with a verdict of guilty. But Texas law states that in some cases, the jury must also decide the defendant's jail sentence as long as both sides are in agreement prior to the trial date. This was one of those cases and we again retired to the jury room to debate on the defendant's jail term. Capital punishment had not been recommended.

Our jury debate ended up with one holdout who apparently just loved the attention he had never received before. Eleven of us wanted to send the man to jail for 60 years, and this juror just wanted to be difficult and wanted less time in jail. After the evening meal, we returned to the jury room for more debate. We reached the point where the judge was about to sequester us for the night and I had even called Audrey to bring me an overnighter when our holdout juror decided he didn't want to spend the night in a hotel room either. We settled for a 45-year sentence. It was probably all academic anyway as the defendant was in his 40's and would remain in the penitentiary all his life anyway, or at least most of it.

The hour now was very late and we had several female jurors that needed transportation home. The judge wisely decided to have us all transported by deputy sheriffs of the Dallas County Sheriff's Department So like all the other jurors, I hopped into a radio car and we headed for home. I was again comfortable in my old environment, listening to the usual cop chatter on the radio. Some squad car was calling for backup and others were responding. And Lonesome George got homesick. Homesick for the streets. In my 30 years on the job, I had spent the last half of them in a supervisory or management position, flying a desk. Although I had enjoyed my role in management, I'd always felt a little cheated missing out on all the action. In fact when with U.S. Treasury, the few times I had joined my people on the street as Chief, I had been chastised for it. Washington, D.C said they were not paying me that kind of money to be on the street. But I still missed what I called grass roots enforcement and it all came flooding back to me.

The following week I applied for a Reserve Deputy Sheriff's position and was accepted. They told me they would not be sending me to their Sheriff's Academy as it would be a waste of time and I would only be taking up space. With my ten years in Texas, I was very familiar with federal criminal law but a little rusty to say the least on the Texas Criminal Code. I hit the law library at nearby Southern Methodist University for a while and then passed the state test for Peace Officer. Old Lonesome George was back on the streets again and loving it. Audrey was not so thrilled, believe me. So we compromised. I would work a couple of days a week and no night work if I could avoid it. Its been working for fourteen years now.

TWENTY-SEVEN

Dallas County is the second largest county in Texas, Harris County which is the Houston area, being the largest. Dallas County covers about 902 square miles with a population of a little over a million people. The Sheriffs Department has about 350 sworn deputies plus 950 Detention Service Officers (jailers) who are not sworn but work the county's four jails. Jail population runs about 6,000 inmates on a regular basis. It's quite an operation. Sworn officers work the usual county law enforcement functions such as Patrol, Warrant Execution, Bailiff, Civil, Narcotics, Criminal Investigation and Crime Scene. Some sworn deputies are still working in the jails but most of them are in a supervisory capacity. Recently Dallas County Sheriffs Department added a Traffic Division to assist local departments in covering the various interstate highways in the county. Although there are a few Reserve Officers with prior law enforcement experience, most are civilians with other jobs who are interested in police work. They are volunteers and receive no compensation. A minimum of 16 hours a month is required. They are allowed to work all functions except Narcotics and Criminal Investigation Division. With my background I probably could have had a waiver but I never pursued it. When I was first sworn in, Reserve Deputies were required to work jail visitation. I hated it. They finally did away with this requirement.

To get back into what I've always referred to as "grass roots law enforcement," I thought it would be prudent to work at least one shift in one of the jails. Other than putting people in one, I really hadn't had all that much exposure in this area and keeping in mind the possibility of quelling a riot or a hostage situation sometime, I thought it was wise to get a little exposure. Although the people working the jails were very helpful, one shift was enough for me. It just wasn't my bag. I then decided to work a day shift in their Patrol Division. The Sunnyvale substation was the closest to me. Sunnyvale is a suburb of Dallas and a delightful community. It does not have its own police department but contracts out to the Dallas County Sheriff for coverage. Like most cities and towns, Sunnyvale has a little pocket not considered very attractive. But for the most part, it is a fairly affluent community with many attractive homes and some beautiful ranches complete with horses and longhorn steers. The problem I had with Sunnyvale was there was very little crime there. I initially worked a day shift with one of the regular deputies and during the entire shift, we had one house burglary with no witnesses and no investigative leads. I ended up interviewing a few neighbors and watching Crime Scene people dust for fingerprints.

After convincing Audrey it would be a one shot deal, I worked the same patrol area on the evening shift. Other than backing up a couple of officers in neighboring communities, my biggest challenge was staying awake. I decided this wasn't my cup of tea either. I needed to find my niche as a Reserve Officer so the Warrants Execution Division was next on my list. Because of the potential danger and need for prior street experience, very few Reserve Officers work Warrants Execution, but it looked like real police work to me.

TWENTY-EIGHT

Of all the other law enforcement functions, the execution of criminal warrants can be one of the trickiest of all assignments. There is always some potential danger lurking. Although officers may have a criminal warrant at any given address for any particular individual, be it a felony or misdemeanor, they never know just who is behind that door. Deputies can be executing a simple warrant for a probation violation on a $50 Theft of Check case and find a felony fugitive wanted out of state for Murder behind the door. And that felon will assume they are after him or her. Deputies must conduct themselves cautiously with a "strictly business" demeanor without giving the "storm trooper" image which can often trigger wanted people and others to become violent or at least hostile. This is especially true in our larger cities and heavy urban areas prone to such behavior. The execution of criminal warrants requires experienced officers.

The Warrants Execution Division in the Dallas County Sheriffs Department is quite an operation. There are about 50 deputies or investigators assigned to two shifts. They work in two person squads and the shifts are from 6:00 AM to 2:30 PM and 2:30 PM to 11:00 PM, Shifts alternate every two weeks which can be very demanding physically in itself, let alone frustrating in planning one's personal life. Deputies are assigned to Warrants Execution by their request and come from other assignments such as Patrol, Bailiff, Jail or other duties. Rarely a deputy who has just graduated from their academy is ever assigned to Warrants Execution Division. Upon assignment there investigators train for six months, spending two months each with three OJT Instructors (On the Job Training). A few don't make it.

The division has a safety record second to none nationwide, probably due to their approach, attitude and intensive training. In Texas almost all warrants issued by the courts go directly to the various Sheriffs Departments for execution and in Dallas County, each two person squad carries an average of 250 to 300 active warrants in its inventory at any given time. They are mostly felony warrants as very little priority is given to misdemeanors. But of course they too have to be executed. In some cases, local constables help out. Usually city traffic warrants are executed by city or town police officers. Under normal conditions, a two person Warrant Squad can make anywhere from two to five arrests a shift, depending on the distance from their assigned district to the central lockup where all prisoners are processed, including those coming from the U.S. Immigration Service and those from other counties and states. It can be a very time consuming process at times, especially when the person who was arrested needs to see a medical person before being admitted to "Central Intake."

In Texas, like any other state, probable cause must be established before officers can enter a dwelling. A principal residence must be established and reasonable belief that the wanted person is in the dwelling is also in order. Officers must identify themselves and when all efforts have been made to get the inhabitants to open the door voluntarily, forced entrance is made, usually with a battering ram. In Dallas County it is now the policy to have a Sergeant and at least two backup squads on sight. This is only for felony warrants, not misdemeanors. Extra body armor, including helmets are now donned by all. I can personally testify folks that in Texas, where summer temperatures can well exceed 100 degrees, this makes life insufferable but with extra protection, a lot safer. When I first started, no supervisor was required and the only protection we had were the vests we routinely wore.

Many addresses listed on criminal warrants are not valid. Either the wanted person listed on the warrant deliberately gave an invalid address initially or he or she does not have any permanent address. This can be frustrating. If the wanted person cannot be located and his or her absence can be attributed to a legitimate source such as a relative, a landlord' or a subsequent owner, the deputies may "at large" it, taking it off their inventory. But the warrant forever remains on the computer until executed or withdrawn by the court. Usually the wanted person will be arrested for another crime and a valid address will be established.

Normally, one of the two investigators in the Warrant Squad will go to the front door of a dwelling and keep in touch via radio while the other deputy gets set at the back door. Wanted persons have a tendency to flee from the back when they know there is an officer at their front door, even though the squad car or cruiser is parked two or three doors down the roadway. The investigator covering the back of the dwelling must always be aware of a Pit Bull, a Rottweiler or some other such animal, lurking in the backyard.

Usually officers can work around this problem or occasionally must use pepper spray. But it's not the dog's fault as it is only protecting its owner's property and cannot differentiate between a burglar or a police officer.

Do wanted persons run? You bet they do. They run and they hide. They hide under the bed, in a closet, in an attic and under the house when there is no cellar. Sometimes it's almost laughable. Just picture yourself watching a person who has crawled into an attic and falls though the sheetrock with legs dangling down into the ceiling below. A wanted person has been found in a dryer and even in a locked automobile trunk. When gaining entrance to a dwelling with a felony warrant, officers are allowed to search without a search warrant as long as it's a surface search to ensure their safety from weapons and other dangers. Drugs are often found on the premises. When a person other than the wanted person answers the door claiming the wanted person is not there, he or she is usually cautioned about a charge of Hindering Apprehension being filed if appropriate. In Texas, that is a felony. And speaking of drugs, it is estimated in Dallas County, 85% of the crimes being arrested for on warrants can in some way be attributed to the use of illegal drugs. It is not uncommon to execute a criminal warrant at a drug house. However, deputies are usually quite familiar with their assigned districts and know where most of the drug houses are in their area. Extra precaution is always taken and a backup squad is called for when any potential danger to officers is prevalent. Anyone who has ever worked narcotics cases is painfully aware of hitting a drug lab. One never knows when the stuff will explode. Combined with the mentality of a dope dealer, it is always wise to take extra precaution.

TWENTY-NINE

The first time I worked the day shift in Warrants Execution, the Lieutenant-in-Charge, familiar with my background, said that he had a one deputy squad that day, his partner being on sick leave. He asked me to fill in, making it a regular two-deputy squad. Sounded good to me. Shortly thereafter, a squad car rolled up and I met an investigator we will call Chuck Skillman. Chuck, as I was to learn later, turned out to be a legend in his own time. He and I started hitting houses in an attempt to serve felony warrants. Chuck seemed to have an aversion for misdemeanor warrants and we concentrated on warrants for dope dealers, robbery, aggravated assault and murder. At about mid-morning, Investigator Mike Ramirez and his partner in another squad called us for a backup. They had a warrant for a guy wanted for aggravated assault and he had let it be known that if the cops ever came after him, he would take at least one with him when he went down. That, for everybody signaled a possible shootout and of course it got our attention.

Upon arriving at the scene we were told that the wanted person was in the house but would not open the front door. I was asked to cover the back, lest the wanted person attempted to escape that way as so often wanted persons do. Although currently, all Warrant Investigators wear Class B uniforms readily identifying them as law enforcement officers, in those days a shirt, tie and suit were required. It was a bitterly cold January day. As I stood there in my overcoat (thank Heaven) in a backyard full of frozen mud behind the only tree in sight for cover, I began to have second thoughts. Ramariz had asked me if I had my vest on and I replied that I had. He then retrieved a shotgun from the trunk of his squad car, threw it to me reminding me it was loaded. Now personally, I never was really comfortable with shotguns. Although they played a certain psychological advantage on a person attempting to escape or assault you, both hands are required to use the weapon and I always felt somewhat restricted.

So there I stood with my teeth chattering, dressed for church so to speak, behind the only tree in sight for cover, waiting for some clown to come out and shoot me. I can recall looking up in the sky and saying to myself, "Why me?" I could almost hear the reply coming down. "Isn't this what you wanted, George?" Yes. I guess it was. At any rate, the wanted person realized we weren't going to go away, finally opened the front door and surrendered. He was arrested and Chuck and I returned to our assigned district to hit more houses.

I continued to work with Chuck Skillman as I did with all the other squads when they worked days. But Skillman was a magnet for trouble. I could almost count on getting into a foot chase or some other situation when I rode with Skillman.

I can recall on one occasion, Dallas PD was chasing a couple of guys who'd just robbed a bank and had hopped up on the interstate. Of course Skillman couldn't resist a good chase and had our squad car up to 115 MPH before a police helicopter finally zeroed in on the subjects and they were apprehended. Skillman finally pulled over to make a telephone call and I got out to stretch my legs. I noticed one of the squad car's front tires was almost bald. Wonderful! Lonesome George squeaks by another one.

In another situation, Skillman and I located a wanted person on the third floor of an apartment house in Dallas. Since we had a backup squad with us we made a forced entry. In an act of desperation, the wanted person actually jumped out of a third story window. But Skillman was right after him jumping too and the foot chase was on. When we finally apprehended him, he looked up at Skillman and said, "Man, are you crazy? Jumping out of a third story window like that? I sure never thought you'd do that!" There was just no way to get away from Skillman. As for the wanted person's comment about Skillman being crazy, I was beginning to think he may have had a point.

Then one day I earned the medal that no law enforcement officer really wants. The Purple Heart. Guess who my partner happened to be? Right. Chuck Skillman. However I will say this. Chuck had nothing to do with the injuries I sustained. As it happened, we had a felony warrant on a parole violator who had done time for Armed Robbery. At the time, his brother was doing time for murder in Oklahoma. Nice family. We had received information that the wanted person was working in a warehouse in Carrollton, Texas and because of his lengthy criminal record we had a back-up squad with us. Discreet inquiry with the wanted person's supervisor revealed that his shift ended at 1:00 PM and he usually left by the back door of the building facing a parking lot. We had a mug shot of him with us which is always wise.

We hid our squad cars as much as possible and shortly after 1:00 PM the wanted person came out the door as we expected. He was immediately arrested and I handcuffed him with his hands behind his back. There was no resistance from him at that time as usually it was all over by then. But not this time.

As I was placing the prisoner in the right back seat of our squad car and Skillman was getting behind the wheel, this clown suddenly bolted from me and started running across the parking lot with his hands still cuffed behind his back. All I could think of i^^-my $30 handcuffs were getting away from me. The foot chase was on and at the time I was wearing loafers and I ran right out of them. I hit the macadam at about 7 MPH face down and out like a light. When I came to, the prisoner had been apprehended. He was returned to the penitentiary but as I understand it, not before being severely lectured on his attitude toward police. I ended up with a concussion and eight stitches in my head. You can rest assured that was the last time I ever wore loafers on the job.

Over the years, Skillman had developed a network of informants. Most were bondsmen whose clients had jumped bail and they were trying to get their money back. When I worked with another shift and Skillman was off duty, it was not uncommon to get a call from him with information on a wanted person's whereabouts. He would meet us in his own personal car at the address and the wanted person would be located and arrested.

But like so many other officers, Skillman became paranoid about the job and it eventually consumed him. Alcohol may have played a part and maybe even drugs but I hated to think so. He began to have hallucinations and tell weird stories about people following him. The Sheriffs Department tried to help, offering him medical and psychiatric aid to save his retirement that he would have been eligible for in another year but they couldn't get to him. His coworkers pleaded with him but to no avail. He finally resigned and drew all his retirement money out, which was substantial. I understand he blew it all shortly thereafter at the casinos in nearby Louisiana. The last time I looked, there were several outstanding warrants on him in Dallas County for Theft by Check. A very sad story indeed.

THIRTY

As previously mentioned, when working Warrants Execution, be aware. Wanted persons run, hide and as a matter of fact lie a lot too. They simply don't want to go to jail. Or should I say in most cases, don't want to go back to jail. I was involved in one situation where the wanted person, having no attic in the house, decided to hide under the dwelling. It had recently rained and there were about six inches of mud under there. I swear this guy weighed 250 pounds and it took three of us to get him dislodged. We had to practically hose him down before getting him into our squad car.

I can also recall executing a misdemeanor warrant in Irving, Texas with Investigator Wayne Latour. It was at an apartment complex and the guy lived on the third floor. Latour took the front door and I covered the back which was a balcony three floors up with me on the ground watching. Since it was a misdemeanor case we had no authority to make a forced entry if there was no response and we wouldn't have had probable cause anyway. But in this case, the wanted person saw Latour through the peephole and decided to leave by the back balcony. He was about to jump and I pulled out my weapon just for effect and yelled, "Don't jump!" I could just envision this guy jumping three floors down and breaking a leg. Latour and I would then have to spent the rest of our tour of duty babysitting this clown at the county hospital and we didn't need that. Anyway, he didn't jump down. He jumped up. Right onto the roof. Swell! Although the roof was flat, neither Latour nor I wanted any part of a foot chase on a roof, especially on a misdemeanor case. We eventually talked him down, he surrendered and we put him in the back seat of our squad car. On the way to the jail, he started to cry. I always hate to see a grown man cry so I calmed him down, telling him it was only a misdemeanor case and he would probably be out of jail in a few days. He finally settled down.

Another challenge which deputies face when assigned to the Warrants Execution Division is executing mental illness warrants. These warrants also require a backup squad as officers really don't know the mental condition of the patient who is being transported to the hospital for care. It can range from an elderly person suffering from Alzheimer disease, a raging maniac, or simply a "menopause Minnie" so to speak. It is not uncommon for a mentally disturbed person to rant and rave all the way to the hospital and upon arrival there, remain quiet and peaceful during the admitting process.

Not long ago. Deputies Paul Patterson and Wilson Womack, along with a backup squad, were attempting to serve a warrant on a mentally disturbed man. It was on the evening shift. As they approached the house, he suddenly appeared on the porch with a rifle, shot Patterson in the leg and Womack in the head. Deputy Womack would not be with us today if the bullet had been a half inch closer to his skull. Deputies still managed to apprehend the man and Deputy Womack received the Sheriffs Medal of Honor for his performance. I was not present when the shooting occurred but the next day I had to drive their squad car to the shop for cleanup. The windshield was covered with blood and it made me stop and think a little but I tried not to dwell on it too much. Both Patterson and Womack are Sergeants now. I always enjoyed Womack's remark when his coworkers kidded him occasionally when he made a slight error. Womack would always respond with, "I have an excuse. I've been shot in the head."

Dope houses can also be a real challenge to deputies working Warrants Execution. But they can also be quite interesting and rewarding. I remember when my squad was called to back up another squad who had a warrant for a person wanted for Possession of Cocaine with Intent to Sell. Not a bad neighborhood or dwelling but obviously a possible dope house. Usually when warrant officers suspect more than one person is inside a dwelling that might be a dope house, they call for a backup squad. There is always the possibility that other persons with outstanding warrants are in the house too but they cannot be run on the computer without identification. Such was this case. The person we had a warrant for was inside the house and was arrested. There was another person there too with an outstanding drug warrant. We handcuffed them both and seated them on the living room sofa while we conducted a surface search of the adjacent rooms for other persons or anything that might be a danger to us.

Boy, did we ever fall into something. There were illegal drugs all over the place. Even in the kitchen cabinet. And stolen goods too. In the garage we found several television sets and computers that appeared to have been stolen and were being fenced, as well as a high priced motorcycle which had been reported stolen.

As procedure dictated, when discovering illegal drugs or possible stolen merchandise, we contacted our Criminal Investigation Division people who arrived on the scene shortly thereafter. So while we made sure our two persons under arrest were secure on the sofa, CID investigators began their laborious task of recording the inventory to be seized.

Then the telephone rang. Usually under those circumstances, officers just let the telephone ring but fortunately one of our CID Investigators answered it with a, "Yeah?" He heard male voice on the other end of the line say, "We've got some stuff for you." The CID Investigator said, "Wacha got?" The voice replied, "A bunch of computers." The CID Investigator wisely responded, "Well bring them on over." The male voice replied, "Okay. We'll be right there."

We then quickly moved all marked and unmarked squad cars out of view of the house and about 15 minutes later, two males arrived in the driveway with a pickup truck full of computers. They knocked on the door and were immediately arrested for Possession of Stolen Goods.

In addition to the stolen merchandise and illegal drugs, there was a substantial amount of cash in the house. We seized everything and logged it all in as evidence. It was then up to the court to decide whether the person we had arrested for possession of illegal drugs with intent to sell and the owner of the house, would get any of the seized property back. Probably not. If the owner or owners of the stolen property had reported any merchandise stolen, it would eventually be returned to them. The Internal Revenue Service had also been contacted. Their procedure was to file a Jeopardy Assessment against the defendant based upon what IRS estimated his illegal ome would amount to, considering the cash that was seized. One more loser down the drain with no loss to society. There is some satisfaction in our business, after all.

One of the aspects I've always liked about grass roots law enforcement was that from hour to hour, one never knew what to expect. One day I was working Warrants Execution with Investigators Larry Smith and John Jameson, both extremely capable officers. We were attempting to execute a felony warrant in East Dallas and happened to drive by an alley. There were three Dallas PD squad cars parked there, all with their strobe lights flashing. We stopped and offered our assistance. They said they had just received a call reporting a possible attempted house burglary and gave us the description of the suspect which had been given by a neighbor. We started to assist with our own foot search.

About four or five minutes later, we saw a guy coming down the alley toward us who answered the description of the suspect. We immediately spread eagled him on the ground, cuffed him and searched him for possible weapons. He had a six-inch butcher knife hidden on his person. We handed him over to Dallas officers who were quite pleased and returned to our squad car to resume our search for wanted persons.

Smith was driving and we hadn't gone but a few blocks when we reached a main thoroughfare. As we passed a small fried chicken restaurant, we noticed a man entering the front door. He had a gun in his hand. Oh, oh! Trouble there. Smith immediately parked our squad car behind the restaurant, out of view and we peeked through a side window. The man we had seen entering was standing in the restaurant with a revolver in his hand talking to another man who appeared to be the restaurant's manager. He looked rather upset as did two other people who appeared to be employees. There were no customers in there that we could see. We decided not to go into the restaurant as to do so might trigger a shootout causing a civilian to catch a stray bullet. We sure didn't want that. So Smith and Jameson waited outside the main entrance while I continued to peek through the side window. I really couldn't see much from my position without disclosing my presence. In a few minutes the suspect emerged with two canvas moneybags. There was no weapon in view. He was immediately put on the ground face down, handcuffed and his weapon retrieved. We found proper identification on him identifying him as a firefighter from the nearby city of Richardson, Texas. He held a valid Texas license to carry a concealed weapon. We hadn't apprehended an armed robber at all. We'd captured the complainant or victim.

It seemed that the firefighter owned a carwash establishment about a block away. He had gone there to collect the money that had been deposited. He collected the money, put it in two canvas moneybags and returned to his pickup truck where he placed it on the driver's seat. He then returned to the carwash to make sure he had secured everything and started walking back to his pickup truck. He observed two males reaching into the cab and grab the moneybags. They saw him coming and took off on foot toward the restaurant with the moneybags. He retrieved a weapon from his truck and ran off on foot after them. Of course we didn't see the two thieves enter the restaurant. All we saw was a man with a gun enter. The thieves had entered the restaurant, dropped the moneybags on the floor and had fled out a side door. The manager said he had never seen either of them before. Of course the firefighter, a little shaken up by now, was released, his weapon returned with our apology and was put on his way back to his pickup truck. We then searched the neighborhood but of course the two thieves were long gone. I'd had a real busy day. I reminded myself that when I got home, I would check my calendar for a full moon that night.

THIRTY ONE

While working with Warrants Execution Division, I got into my first fight in years. At least it was a fight to me anyway. I was with Investigators Shane Chaddick and Darrell Watson, two solid guys and a pleasure to work with. We were attempting to serve a felony warrant on a female in Dallas. As we approached her primary residence, a rather modest dwelling, Watson went to the rear of the house to watch the backdoor while Chaddick and I went to the front. After knocking several times, a white male opened the door. He was in his early 40's and very muscular, obviously in good shape. We asked if this was the principal residence of the wanted person and he replied that it was but that she had left for Abilene two weeks ago and he was staying there as a guest. We told him we had a felony warrant for her arrest and that we needed to come in and verify her not being there. He said, "You're not coming in here," which of course was a big mistake. Chaddick told him to face the porch wall with his hands behind his back. This assured officer safety. The man became hostile and the fight was on. Now Chaddick is 35 years old, six feet tall, weighs 220 pounds and works out continually. But it took the two of us several minutes to subdue him and we even had to use two sets of handcuffs before we finally got him under control. We couldn't mace him because the porch was only about six feet square and we would have ended up spraying each other. Watson, still watching the backdoor, was unaware of all this activity and when contacted by radio, came around to the front door. I then held the male by his handcuffs while Chaddick and Watson searched the interior of the residence for the wanted female. She was hiding in a bedroom closet and we arrested her on the felony warrant. We also arrested her male companion for Hindering Apprehension. Because of his previous record he got five years. All this jerk had to say was, "This isn't my house. Come on in and look around." But as I've previously mentioned, we don't normally deal with rocket scientists. I thought to myself, "George, you're getting to be too old to be rolling around on the floor with some dirt bag." But of course, I didn't really have much choice. We never do, do we?

I had worked Warrants Execution with Investigators Mike Jesttes and Greg Artisi a lot. They were known by their coworkers as "Batman and Robin." On the street they were especially aggressive but effective and fun to work with. Both are now Sergeants and Jesttes has had a tour as our Range Officer.

On June 27,1990, Artisi had been off duty so l joined Jesttes, making it a two-investigator squad. Part of our district was in Irving, Texas, a major city adjacent to Dallas. It was approaching lunchtime and Jesttes handed me a teletype alerting us that Abilene, Texas Police were looking for 24 year old Andrew Cantu, wanted for a triple murder in that city about two weeks previous. They had reason to believe Cantu might be hiding out at his sister's apartment in Irving. Mike pointed out to me that the teletype was two weeks old and had probably been "beaten to death" by other squads by now and the information was probably worthless. He suggested that we make a quick stop at Cantu's sister's apartment, just in case and then break for lunch. Sounded good to me.

We rolled up at the apartment complex and checked out her apartment which was located on the second floor of the complex. We knocked on the door and no answer. On the way back to our squad car we saw the apartment complex manager walk by and Jesttes casually asked him if he had seen anyone of Cantu's description at that particular second floor apartment. The manager replied, "Oh yeah. He's in there. At least from who you've described, I've seen him." Jesttes and I looked at each other and immediately reacted. I flew around back to cover the balcony of the apartment and Jesttes ran back up to Cantu's sister's apartment. Jesttes started banging on the front door so hard I could see the glass at the rear of the apartment shake.

Then two officers in an Irving police car stopped to see what was going on. We asked them to assist and they said their department's policy was not to enter a dwelling without a search warrant. Jesttes was disturbed with this information and said, "All we have is this teletype. If you can't back me up, the least you can do is relieve my partner here so he can back me up." They readily agreed.

Somehow we got the door open. Maybe the manager let us in. I don't recall. We found Cantu hiding under the bed, unarmed. He was arrested and transported to our Central Intake for processing. By now the news media had arrived with their television cameras and we made the evening news. His bail was set at $1,000,000. We then called Abilene PD to notify them that we had Cantu in custody and they replied they would make arrangements to have the prisoner transported back to Abilene for arraignment. The Abilene officer then casually asked Jesttes if Cantu had his Uzi on him as they suspected. For those of you who are not familiar with an Uzi, it is a submachine gun and very lethal. Jesttes became rather upset and said Cantu did not and if Abilene PD had information that Cantu was in possession of an Uzi, why wasn't that information included in the teletype? The officer rather apologetically said he was sorry. Of course by now everyone knew that somebody at Abilene PD had messed up. Once again Lonesome George had dodged a bullet, literally. As I've said before, the Good Lord watches over cops and drunks.

Epilogue

Well, that about wraps it up. If you've gotten this far, I hope you now have a little insight of a cop's life that didn't come out of Hollywood or off your TV screen. I have been particularly fortunate in having been exposed to just about every aspect of our occupation. Like in every other profession, I've had my bad days too but overall, other than having eight stitches in my head on one occasion, I have survived unscathed. At least up until now anyway. I have enjoyed it immensely and will continue to be out there as long as my health allows. I guess I'm just a glutton for punishment. These days, our younger officers keep me young too. I don't jump six-foot fences anymore. I keep them down to two or three feet at the most. When I feel I am a risk to any officer out there I'll probably find something a little less stressful. But at least for now, they still keep calling me so I'll still be out there on the street.

Looking back at it all, I've been very blessed. I've had a wonderful marriage for over 50 years now, a loving wife and daughter and have even survived a bout with cancer. I was so fortunate in finding my calling early in life. So many people have not been that lucky. Although there are some people I have put in jail over the years that might disagree, I hope I have made a small contribution to society. It has been extremely rewarding for me.